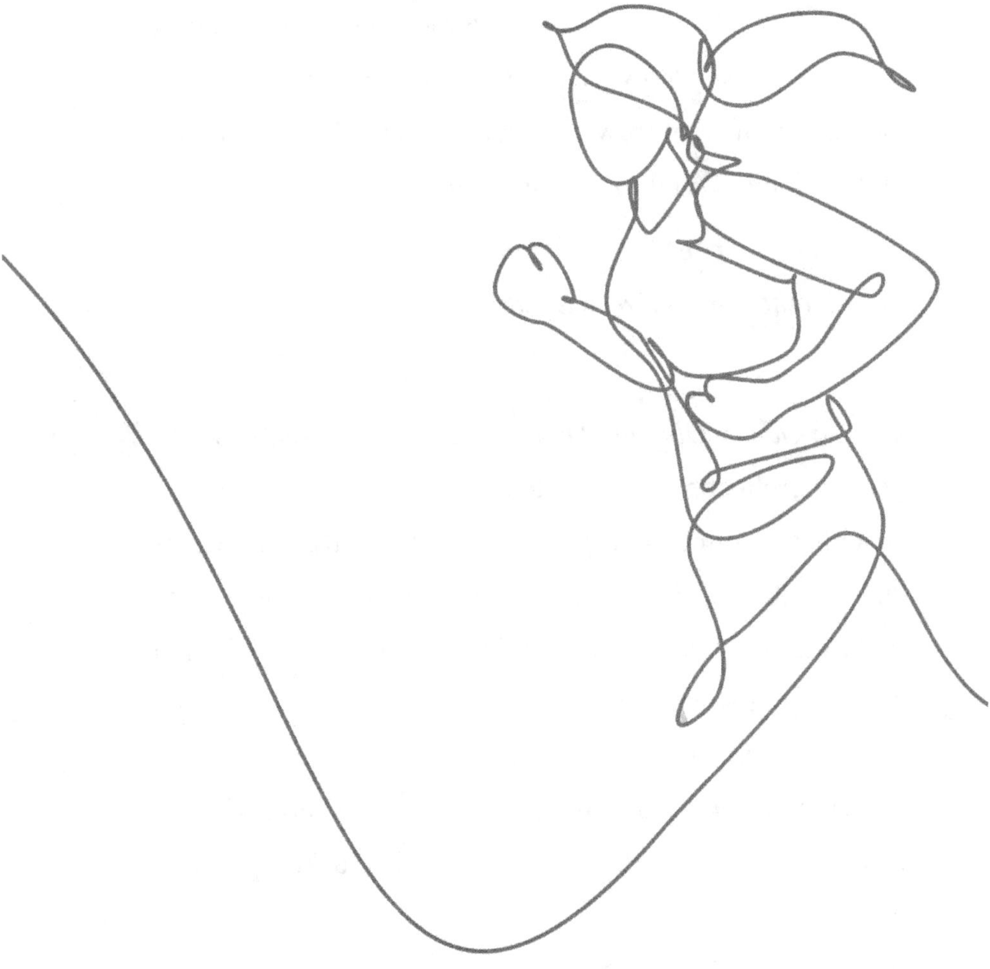

The Olympic games are just one of a few elements of ageless, worldwide culture. Buried beneath the goodwill and world unity we yearn for every four years, are untold stories and truths which athletes and spectators of the "modern era" need to know. Janice Kehler has intensely researched and bravely recounted some of these stories. Many of the accounts within *Ode to Olympic Dreams* were well known; but Janice is among the first authors willing to recount these stories with objectivity and realism. "Glory" has a certain meaning when it comes to the Olympics. However, glory alone cannot define our perception of what truly are "games." This fascinating read is a "must" for all "Olympic-philes."

Carla Albano
*Author of **Soul of a Swimmer***

I found *Ode to Olympic Dreams* a delightful combination of personal reflections from a dream-filled young athlete and a rich history of the Olympic movement. Jan Kehler weaves an enjoyable fabric out of the history of competing narratives within sport; "being your best" and "win at any cost". In the sociology of sport, it is often said that sport is our peacetime war. Whether we choose to compete fairly or unfairly is an ethical question for all time for all of us, in sport and life. This read studies that question deeply with the backdrop of Olympic dreams.

Gary M. Sater, PhD
Clinical Sport Psychologist (retired)

As an avid journal writer, I at once felt a connection with Kehler's work. Coupled by the fact that she grew up in Winnipeg, Manitoba, as I did, and was referring to places familiar to me, a bond was created for me as a reader partaking in her work as the author. It is true, your connective experience with the author and compositions may differ from my own. However, what you will discover, as you navigate alongside her life journey of Olympic endeavors, as she openly and vulnerably shares her firsthand experiences, successes, setbacks, and her impressions on world sporting events and Olympic games, that you too will acquire your unique connection and be drawn into what you will read. Perhaps you, dear reader, like me, have never experienced the highs and lows of striving for Olympic glory. But the joy of movement, physical literacy, effortlessness, and athletics are features we have all encountered and sensed, and therefore, have allowed us to appreciate the value of vanquishing our staunchest competitor, ourselves.

James P. Speidel
Community Schools Partnership, Surrey School District
Surrey, British Colombia, Canada

Ode to Olympic Dreams

By Janice P. Kehler MSc, MA

To my grandchildren, Bryce, Sloane, and Ansel, as they venture forth to explore the joy of their athleticism.

To athletes and spectators whose untold stories, inspired by the creativity of Coubertin's ideals, reveal the wonder of all that one can be...

Alongside the spirit of learning from the past and looking to the future, I honor the traditional lands and historical legacies of all Indigenous peoples and communities across Canada and the USA.

Ode to Olympic Dreams
Author: Janice P. Kehler
Editor: Taylor Brien
Proofreader: Lyda Rose Haerle, Megan Moyer
Cover Design: Nicole Wurtele
Interior Layout: Griffin Mill

All images are courtesy of Janice P. Kehler unless otherwise noted.

IOC legal gives permission to quote the principles of Olympism as written in the Charter of the International Olympic Committee (IOC), 2020.

ISBN: 979-8-9881891-2-1

PUBLISHED BY CG SPORTS PUBLISHING

AN IMPRINT OF
NICO 11 PUBLISHING & DESIGN
MUKWONAGO, WISCONSIN
MICHAEL NICLOY, PUBLISHER

www.nico11publishing.com

Quantity order requests can be emailed to:

mike@nico11publishing.com

Printed in The United States of America

Contents

Ode to Sport

O sport you are Justice! The perfect fairness which men seek in vain in their social institutions rises around you of its own accord...

O sport you are Joy! At your call the flesh makes holiday and the eyes smile; the blood flows free and strong in the arteries. Thought's horizon grows lighter and more clear...

Written by Baron de Coubertin
Journal of Olympic History 14 (May 2006)

CHAPTER ONE

Discovering My Bliss

"I am very glad that even though I was never an
Olympic or World champion, because of *Wide
World of Sports* I am remembered by so many."
Vinko Bogataj

My first memory of the outside world began with words
swirling above my head, scary, fear-filled bits of
faraway sounds, '*crip-ple, crip-pled, crip-pling.*' My sister,
who sat on an adult-sized red chair across from my crib, her
legs dangling, was holding her reader. She opened the book just
as her legs began to swing and her voice rang out, softer words
propelled by her legs. I reached for the top wooden rail of my
crib, covered by a plastic sleeve, and pulled myself upward.
Sounds were within my reach.

My hands squirmed, causing the plastic sleeve to
shift back and forth, clicking softly. Her words rose and fell
while her legs swung. The plastic sleeve butted up against
the headboard, then the footboard of my crib. Swishing and
clicking merged with her sing-song voice, washing over me
just as my toes lifted me upward onto the balls of my feet. A
curious tickle formed near my belly button—a bubble of joy,
clamoring upwards until it reached my mouth.

There was only one thing left to do.

Folding forward, I opened my mouth letting the bubble escape while I sunk my teeth into the taffy-like plastic. Delight shivered up and down my backbone. Again and again, bouncing and gnawing, legs swinging and her voice rising and falling until there were no more pages, no more words, and the reader lay on my sister's lap.

Most days, when my sister read to me, I bounced and chomped, but some days I walked on the balls of my feet; toe-walking back and forth along the crib rails, pausing to sink my teeth into the plastic. It would become a permanent record of joy-filled movement fueled by words.

Years later, in grade school, I ran my finger over the teeth marks as I helped my mother unpack the crib. My aunt and uncle were moving from Texas, where my uncle played professional hockey, to Winnipeg, my hometown. My mother offered to help with their new baby even though she whispered at dinnertime that my aunt and uncle were still not married. Most of the time, the baby slept, but I studied his every move while awake. For my family's sake, I was hoping he would toe-walk. Didn't all babies toe-walk?

Over a decade later, I researched toe-walking as part of my training as a physiotherapist. The facts: toe-walking occurs in 4.9% of children from one to five years of age; first steps happen around the same time as those toddlers that walk flat-footed, and half will quit by the time they are eight years old. Stiff ankles, as adults, were the only consequence. Yet, toe-walkers often underwent exercise regimes, and if that failed, surgical interventions would be considered to allay parental concerns.

My parents feared I would become '*a cripple.*' But my joy in toe-walking outlasted their fears. Eventually, as a young adult, I became part of the stiff ankles club after another physiotherapy student measured my ankle range of motion, and found it to be ten degrees short of normal. My professors frowned at this '*significant finding.*' I shrugged it off. My love of toe-walking had been the entryway to the outside world and to running; stiff ankles were a small price to pay.

I spent my early childhood wanting to be like my two older siblings. My sister and brother could read, and I could not. Kindergarten, a place, my brother had told me, where I would be taught to read, was too expensive. Instead, my mother promised to teach me. She sat me in front of a TV along with a brand-new suitcase of art supplies, and I watched the '*educational children shows,*' while my mother's steam iron hissed, and pounded out the wrinkles in our clothes. At the same time, she chanted, echoing whatever letter was popping up on the TV screen. Sounds ricocheted between us.

As I lay on my back, my hands cradling my head so I could see the TV screen, I felt the energy of my toes digging into the coarsely woven cloth that covered the TV speakers.

'*Ha-ha -ha,*' my mother chanted. My toes wiggled furiously. Her '*oooo,*' and '*iiirt,*' required a slower beat. '*Sh, sh,*' joined with the hiss of her iron, just as my big toe popped free of the cloth and caught the slow wave of her '*oooing.*' Her teaching was fun, and my toes mischievously snuggled deeper into the cloth and then, like a magician pulling a rabbit from a hat, I pulled out the word shoes.

And so it went, words orchestrated by the joy of movement, but this time, the pure joy of toe-walking had been captured by musical sounds that I could tap and slide and wiggle together. Within days, I was feeling the sounds of letters and reading new words, even after her chanting had stopped, after the hiss and thud of her ironing was a distant memory.

By the time I was in grade school, my father and I would eat fresh donuts while watching the *'sport shows'* including the infamous *Wide World of Sports.*

"Spanning the globe," the announcement that called us to attention, "to bring you the constant variety of sport... the thrill of victory... and the agony of defeat... the human drama of athletic competition..."

We studied the images of stylized athletic movements and the spectacular crash of ski jumper Vinko Bogataj. Every week, during the opening montage, trumpets blared, and we held our breaths as Bogataj barreled down the ski jump, miscalculated his take-off, his body catapulting sideways and then falling like a dead weight into a crowd of people. Later, I would learn he suffered only a concussion.

Each week, different sports were reported on. I sat on the floor cross-legged close to the television, barely moving, hypnotized by the effortless flow of well-tuned athletic bodies striving to win. I studied the winners, comparing their abilities to my own know-how in winning the sack and three-legged races at family picnics. I tried to decipher why I always lost to the boys when we raced our bikes to school, and consoled myself remembering that I was regularly the first person picked to play flag football with my brother's friends. I could run faster than the boys and scored a touchdown whenever given a chance.

When the losses of Canadian athletes became apparent, a common occurrence, my legs unfurled, and my body lay flat. Reaching with my feet, I once again embedded my toes into the cloth that covered the television speakers and carefully timed my toe-wiggling to match their athleticism, an imaginary boost to victory.

My father had the opposite body language. He sat in an oversized, pillowed chair. At the peak of action, he leaned towards the TV, throwing his body into wild cheering, teetering on the edge of the chair. When the Canadian athletes lost, he slumped backward, huffing, and gasping, wounded by defeat.

Stories about my father's family, seemingly a cadre of talented athletes *'running as fast as the wind,'* wove themselves through the hours of watching TV. He backed up his claims with vivid descriptions of his brothers, slimmer, muscular, and not saggy like they had been at our summertime family picnics.

Some Saturdays, I worked on becoming an athlete, imagining that I would represent Canada at the Olympics and hear the national anthem play as I stood on the podium—but in what sport? I discovered I could outrun everyone when I played tag. I had taught myself to skate in a straight line and learned that jumping and twirling on skates was nearly impossible. My parents, I decided, had the money for sports; they paid for my swimming lessons. But mostly, I was confident of becoming a graceful, gravity-defying athlete who walked on her toes, certain that all athletes had been toe-walkers at some time in their lives.

Dinnertime conversations dwelled on my toe-walking. My mother declared it '*not normal;*' it could lead to a '*permanent limp.*' She noted my seven years as being the age when I should '*not be babied.*'

Her final argument: we could not afford the special leather shoes that would make me flat-footed.

My father, who always sat at the head of the dinner table, interrupted my mother's fearful talk: "I love to watch her run, winding up from flat foot to tippy toes and then *pouf,* exploding, leaving everyone behind as if they were standing still. She doesn't look like a cripple."

I loved the sound of this made-up word: *pouf,* the hard *P* followed by *ff* a powerful upward hoist and then a smooth forward glide—toe-walking, pouf-ing, running like the wind— an unexpected fusion of words and feeling that had anointed me as special.

No toe-walking inside the house, '*absolutely never,*' became my mother's double-barreled edict. Outside toe-running, not exactly toe-walking, was given a patriarchal okay.

Dinnertime conversations included the whys and wherefores of getting an education: failing at school was unthinkable and getting a good-paying job a worthy life goal. Nuns, old and young, were my first teachers. They demanded that we use our words responsibly: polite words at recess and quiet words in the classroom. Written words the most critical. Those needed to be both meaningful and responsible.

But responsibility was one of many obstacles. In the 1960s, physical education classes for girls were a wavering dictum of the adult world. My mother believed that sports were too much for a young girl's body, women too fragile. It's common sense. She implored me to change my ways, certain that I was on the road to becoming the dreaded '*tomboy.*'

"Exercise produces a sound body that builds a sound mind," I told her, rephrasing the words of Jim McKay. "I've seen girls do sports on TV, and I can do both school and sports, like boys." Silence, the kind of silence that teetered; either I had said something terribly brilliant or terribly wrong.

I forged ahead.

"I ride my bike fast, everywhere; it's why I can rush to the store and buy the ingredients mum has run out of. It's why I ride my bike to school every day, and you don't have to pay for my bus tickets."

"This is true," my father finally said as he broke into a mischievous grin. He had built me a bike out of those discarded by the neighborhood boys and had guessed at the workings of brakes and pedals. My bike ended up being hard to pedal for everyone except me.

"She's fast. I want her to play on my flag football team," said my brother.

"Of course, she should do sports," my older sister chimed in with a sly smile as she began to insist that I be the one always to go to the grocery store for missing ingredients. She was the least athletic of anyone in my family and hated bike riding.

"Okay, okay," my dad said, "don't get carried away." His favored expression when the conversation needed to stop. "You can do sports, but school comes first."

My mother said nothing more about girls and sports.

Later that night, as I cleaned up the dishes from dinner, a truth settled over me, soaking into my pores like butter on hot toast. I toe-walked from table to sink to cupboards and cutlery drawers. Girls could play sports. They already did. A girl's sound body would ensure a sound mind, and sound minds were responsible minds.

Besides, I wanted to feel the thrill of victory. The agony of defeat never entered my mind.

CHAPTER TWO

Olympism...

"...is a philosophy of life, exalting and combining in
a balanced whole the qualities of body, will and mind.
Blending sport with culture and education, Olympism seeks
to create a way of life based on the joy found in effort, the
educational value of good example, social *responsibility*
and respect for universal fundamental ethical principles."
Charter of the International Olympic Committee (IOC), 2020.

S ome of the first books I read were from a set of
encyclopedias that my mother had bought, probably by
saving stamps she earned shopping at our local grocery store—
the one I could ride my bike to in record time. Encyclopedias
were held in high regard by my teachers, especially Sister
Adrian, whose favorite word was '*responsibility.*' Every day
she rolled up her sleeve, the only skin we would see, and wrote
with long sweeping strokes on the chalkboard the rules of
grammar: nouns and verbs, clauses and phrases, periods and
commas, building a story from the ground up by gathering
words into sentences. Learning to write a responsible essay was
to be the culmination of the year we spent together.

I ran my fingers across the shelf of faux leather covers
stopping at the book labeled with the letter *C*, aghast that such

a thick book had so much to say about *C*-words. I added it to
the pile of grammar books and papers on the kitchen table,
getting ready to write my essay for Sister Adrian. The spine
cracked as I opened the book, and flecks of gold fell away from
the pages gilded edges as I hurriedly searched for the word
Coubertin—a man who owned the myth, the declared father
of the modern games by the experts on *Wide World of Sports*.
The French-i-ness of Coubertin echoed as I was careful not
to emphasize the last '*nn*' as I repeated his name with every
turn of the page, instinctively practicing the French accent
that my mother could turn on and off, depending on the social
circumstance. She had grown up in the second-largest French
community in Canada outside of Quebec, and hoped that
someday her three children would learn to speak French.

Finally, I found Coubertin; his exact name was Pierre
de Coubertin. He had a small frame, topped by a grim facial
expression and a funny looking mustache. He looked too
skinny to be athletic, and yet, I assumed that he knew about
the joy of movement and sport. Maybe he knew about toe-
walking. I laughed at how he mocked the idea that wearing
shorts and loose-fitting shirts exposed too many body parts.
I read the story of how Theodore Roosevelt and Coubertin,
who had come to the US to learn about sport in American
universities, had gone camping. I imagined them sitting around
a campfire, just like my family had done the summer before,
while Roosevelt told Coubertin how a sound body makes a
sound mind. The pages of the encyclopedia were certain that

this was '*the idea*,' that inspired his passion for the revival of the ancient Games.

I discovered that he had written a poem, "Ode to Sport," each stanza headed by heroic words like daring, strength, and power. He insisted on athletes wearing national uniforms, teams of athletes from all nations that would cheer for each other, a worldly community of sport. He encouraged posters and sculptures that depicted the muscularity and heroism of ancient (albeit all male) athletes. They had worked hard to be skilled. I translated this into words that I knew would please Sister Adrian: fairness, friendship, and responsibility. The last sentence of my essay fell into place: The Olympics and the demands of sport were responsible for making the world a friendly place.

But I had one big problem. I did not want to include in my essay the fact that Coubertin believed women should not be a part of the Olympic endeavor, or that sports were too taxing and women too fragile. How could I include this when I did not believe it?

"Mr. Coubertin was wrong," I told my parents as we sat at the dinner table. I leaned forward and waved my fork at them. "Is being wrong the same as not being responsible?"

Mother's eating stalled. My father squirmed. I had stumped them.

My father probably answered me emphasizing responsibility over being factually correct. I interpreted his words as being a green light to write what I thought. I eventually wrote that Coubertin was wrong: girls could play sports. They already did. A girl's sound body would ensure a sound mind, and sound minds were responsible minds. Sister Adrian returned my corrected essay with a thick, red smudgy looking check mark beside that paragraph, as if her fountain pen had hovered for a long time shedding its color, its wetness soaking the paper.

Many scholars and historians have researched the life of Coubertin, marrying the facts of his era to the man, who by all appearances, was not an athlete. Amazingly he inspired and ultimately brought to life an international sporting event that spanned the twentieth century and continues into the twenty-first. He was born on January 1, 1863, in Paris, France, to an aristocratic family. By 1896, he had ushered in the revival of a modest, fraught with controversy, Modern Games. Throughout his lifetime he rode the wave of the excitement of sport, the turmoil of his personal life, and the draining of his wealth. He died on September 2, 1937, living in Geneva, Switzerland, alone and penniless. He had the aura of a tragic hero, just like the mythic Greek Olympians, a man of vision who lived and died on the edge of his dreams.

His passion for sport, and the ideals of his Olympism, was never questioned during the era of my watching *Wide*

World of Sports. He was often introduced as the father of the modern Games, while during his lifetime he was addressed as le Rénovateur, a word I translated into a man who likes to renovate, to remodel the playing field of gentlemanly sport. The more I read, thought, and wrote facts into words, as Sister Adrian had taught us, the more I became a disciple of his ideal. The joy of my toe-walking merged with this mysterious and beautiful dream, a grand and enduring idea that mattered to almost everyone in my world. It mattered to Jim McKay as his voice stilled both my father and I when the musical introduction to *Wide World of Sports* blared, and it mattered to the ski-jumper flying high in the sky, crashing, and rolling downhill, only to reappear, eager to continue his competition.

My father admired Coubertin for two reasons: education was vital to build a better life, and sport for girls was common sense. With time, my mother's concerns over sport evolved into admiration over the beauty of the figure skaters, her favorite athletes, especially as they performed their long programs accompanied by classical music. My parents demanded I devote myself to my schoolwork, but also acquiesced to the demands of my training. Dinnertime rituals were rescheduled, and reluctantly, sometimes canceled. Olympism quietly invaded the relationship between me and my parents. An exciting worldly ideal that we thought would be a never-ending adventure.

However, unbeknownst to us, Olympism was also a story of contradictions that did not dwell on the day-to-day struggles to build a better life. On the one hand, Olympism was hope fueled by the joy of athleticism and the fleeting nature of dreams for a better world. However, Coubertin, who had forged a persona as a man of action, was embedded in a world structured by the hierarchies of social class—an aristocracy that was faced with the chaos of the industrial revolution.

He grew up amongst the Parisian upper classes, where he participated in gentlemanly sports like rowing, fencing, boxing, and horseback riding. He was exposed to the competitive world of art through his father's paintings and mediocre success in art competitions, and he studied the classics including the stories of ancient Greek warriors-turned-Olympians, a popular interest amongst Europeans. As a young man he became obsessed with a novel published in 1857, *Tom Brown's School Days,* a popular fictitious rendering of boys learning the ways of men on the rugby fields of British public schools.

But he also might have sensed the turmoil of the social disorder that accompanied the rise of an industrial society. Revolution by the lower classes hovered. I imagine that he felt the resonance between his Olympism and the boxing clubs, founded by Theodore Roosevelt, that improved the lives of underprivileged youth. He embraced the idea that individuals could improve their standing in life, rather than the fate of birth order. He rebelled, eventually joining with the philosophers of his time: a sound body would lead to a sound mind. After failed attempts to follow his father's demands forged by the family's aristocratic life, Coubertin pursued a government appointment responsible for reforming the education of young men in public schools. A dedication to sport as a means to forging a brotherhood among men, but not women, was high on his list of reforms.

Several decades after Coubertin's death, however, the historical record began to reveal the backstory to the dreams of Olympism and the struggles of day-to-day life. One of his solutions was to smother the past with stories and symbols that aligned with his Olympism, while ignoring the facts, or merely choosing to not pursue anything that contradicted his vision. The history of amateurism was one such story that would haunt his Olympism well into the twentieth century.

In 1893, Coubertin was invited to an international conference debating and setting the rules of sport based on the ideal of amateurism. These committees were passionate about keeping both women and the industrial class out of sporting competitions. Professionals (those who made money from their labor, whether training to compete for cash or as a laborer of the lower social class) would invade their world of gentlemen's sport with crass language and tattered attire. Amateurs shaped by their elite upbringing had the moral character needed to uphold the traditions and pleasures of gentlemen-sport.

Coubertin did not record his impressions of the committee's work. In his veiled way of thinking, he reminded his colleagues of the words of Pindar, a lyric poet of ancient

Greece who wrote victory poems to honor heroic Olympians. He praised daring, dedication, and the beauty of victory, shedding a bright light on the superiority of athleticism. Scholars have unearthed the facts: Olympians of Greece were soldiers, men of the lower classes, who were paid to train for competition, and who, if they won, received many favors from the state.

Just as Coubertin ignored the reality that, in his beloved *Tom Brown's School Days*, a young boy's moral character was forged by corporal abuse, his memoirs (at least two of which were written between 1908 and 1931), omitted the systemic cruelty that was also part of the ancient Games, competitions bounded by hundred-year wars. The staging of the ancient Games was merely a temporary truce so that athletes from the warring nations could travel to Greece to compete. Winners were crowned with a wreath made of branches from wild-olive trees. Coubertin saw the crown as a symbol of peace and brotherhood, while many of the ancient Olympians were victorious only after the death of their competitor. It was as if to make his dream a reality, he had to re-invent the past—a grand story that was blinded by his hope for the future.

Eventually, the countless logistical details needed to stage a global event became an impossible reality. So, he began to court entrepreneurs and politicians. He reasoned that the wildly popular world fairs were a logical vehicle to carry his vision onto the playing fields. And so, in 1899, he convinced organizers of the Exposition Universelle in Paris, a world fair that would reveal the daring architecture of the Eiffel Tower, to allow a program of sports demonstrations—a modest concession to targeting the lower social classes without offending the elite sportsman.

In time, those cities that were interested in hosting the Games began to realize the benefits of spectators. Their enthusiasm provided a cheerful soundtrack to the drama of elite competition, while charging for attendance helped to offset the costs of hosting the multiple sporting events. Within a decade, spectators and their money would become a driving force, luring other cities and countries to compete for the privilege to host the Games.

Catering to the needs of the spectators first became evident at the 1912 Stockholm Games, where the organizers hired young boys to call out the schedule of events on the streets of Stockholm. They also arranged for information kiosks to inform the public of the results of competitions by nation. Military bands added to the drama of sport, entertaining spectators with musical interludes as officials hunkered down over their clipboards to determine the winners of the closely fought competitions. No flashy electronic displays, just the delight of marching bands, and the authority of the officials of sport to declare the winner.

Coubertin would have been encouraged by these developments. He would have seen this focus on the spectator as living proof that the lower social classes would learn the virtues of athleticism by watching elite athletes. It was an

example of blending sport with culture and education—a
clarion call for Olympism that would echo throughout the
twentieth century and that would eventually become snared by
the day-to-day realities of building a better life.

In 1920, after the devastation of WWI, the Games
reconvened in Antwerp. At the opening ceremonies, even sixty-
one-year-old Coubertin and his optimistic view of Olympism
could not ignore the failure of sport to deter the horror of war.
He studied the athletes as they marched into the stadium, their
gait was oddly '*lacking elasticity, belonging to aging bodies
and faces.*'

History would reveal astonishing numbers–globally,
fifteen million had died, undoubtedly many who had visions of
becoming an Olympian. The '*Spine of British Olympism,*' the
British army, lost 13% of its recruits, 20% of its officers, and
28% of the military graduates from Oxbridge.

But Coubertin's undying passion for sport was never to
be deterred. Coubertin had long hoped that the Games would
return to Paris. They had first been hosted by the French in
1900 with much controversy. In the competition to host the
1924 Games, Paris was chosen from nine other bids. The
selection of Paris had also been fostered by the growing
acceptance of elite competition as a worthy endeavor by
the higher classes, including an endorsement of the French

Academy of Fine Arts. His life's mission, book-ended by the transformation of Paris culture, had succeeded. It seemed to be the perfect time for Coubertin to retire from the IOC.

The Paris organizers went on to make more significant changes that bolstered Coubertin's ideals. It was the first Games to broadcast competitions on the radio, journalists from all over the world attended, and venues were chosen so that both the sporting elites and lower and middle-classes could attend. In a nod to Coubertin, the 1924 Paris Opening ceremonies was where '*Citius, Altius, Fortius,*' *(Swiftest, Highest, Strongest)* first appeared, a motto that Coubertin had co-opted from a Catholic tradition espoused by the radical Father Didion. Both men held onto the ideal that sport inspired a strong moral order. Competition and physical engagement, principles of Olympism, would remain with the Games well into the twentieth century.

Much to the delight of everyone, before the end of the Paris Games, an Olympic hero emerged by the name of Paavo Nurmi. He earned the name the '*Flying Finn*' with his heroic performances. He ran seven long-distance races in six days, setting world records, and winning his races by large margins. Images of him showed him barefooted on the infield of the stadium, holding his racing shoes, eyes squinting, his face otherwise expressionless. One journalist likened his appearance to a Frankenstein persona, others called him an icon of athletic excellence, a warrior that believed in the no-pain-no-gain philosophy of sport. The strong moral order that Coubertin had prophesied hovered.

The Paris Games also planted the seeds of sporting nationalism. From now on attendance figures (the Paris Games reported the highest number to date) were the mark of success for Olympic officials. Spectators' interest in athletic heroes spread as fast as the journalists could report on their victories. Courage on the battlefield of competition was an oft-repeated phrasing. Pride, a stubborn persistence to win, and to overcome adversity, became aligned with national character and civic duty—a countries medal count, a metric still reported on in today's international world of sport—deemed evidence of the superiority of nations.

By 1928, countries sent not only athletes to compete, but also student-athletes who entertained spectators with sports demonstrations. Coubertin had met Carl Diem at a meeting of the Olympic Congress in Lausanne in 1912. They had formed a close bond over the ideals of Olympism. Subsequently, Diem founded the German Sport University, and it was his students that were then invited to put on a display of their athletic talents. A day of sport demonstrations would have been a proud moment, probably enthusiastically attended by both Diem and Coubertin. Teaching and demonstrating the skills of sport has become a mainstay of the global sporting culture. As if watching sport, one could be inspired. In my grade school, during the 1960s, end of year sports demonstrations became a popular ritual attended by my parents. The same for my daughter, in the late 1980s, a ritual that blended music, dance and well-coordinated marching between gym equipment. Her classmates would then form into columns and demonstrate the sending and receiving of hoops, balls, and brightly colored bean bags.

One of Diem's students, Bruno Balke, had been inspired by his father to pursue a career in physical education, to be the best-that-he-could-be and to guide others toward both physical and mental achievements. Balke had grown up in Austria to a hard-working family that embraced gymnastics and physical activity, the Vienna woods their playground. His father was a physical education teacher who had also fueled his son's curiosity about the physiology and biology of the moving body. Balke as a young man embraced an ambitious collegiate career under Carl Diem's tutelage, and in time would begin medical studies.

Diem was Balke's hero. He followed his training dictums religiously, hoping to compete in the 1932 Games in LA. However, at the last moment, he was declared a non-amateur, ineligible because he had been paid to teach and train students and athletes. At that time, he had registered performances that positioned him as fourth-best in the world. Balke wrote in his autobiography that he believed that he had a chance to stand on the podium. The unruly disconnects of Olympism were coming alive. Balke had embraced the ideals of a sound body leads to a sound mind, he was responsible and dedicated and yet deemed unworthy to compete, his unworthiness determined by the elitism that Olympism had fostered.

Diem had started out as a sports journalist, and then quickly rose to leadership positions as a sport administrator. In the 1936 Games in Berlin, he organized the first torch relay, which began at Mount Olympia in Athens Greece and ended in the state-of-the-art Olympic stadium in Berlin. It was a glorious moment, cementing the trans-historical myth Coubertin had crafted—a romantic connection to heroism and daring and the physical superiority of men.

In the world of Nazism, Diem was considered a half-Jew because his wife's grandmother was Jewish. But his usefulness to Adolf Hitler and his political agenda for the Games spared him. In contrast, by 1937, Coubertin was penniless, in ill health and living alone in Paris. His good friend Diem was supporting him financially by way of his connections to the German government. One wonders what they would have talked about as letters and money were exchanged: the brutality of WWI that they had witnessed, the rising passions for antisemitism, the formation of global alliances that foretold the possibility of another world war, or the disconnect between the dedication to athleticism by Balke, their star-pupil, and his disqualification due to his working-class status, a violation of amateurism.

Were they even aware that they had been manipulated by the ambitious Hitler? That Olympism had in fact been co-opted to demonstrate German superiority?

Eleven months before his death, Coubertin was wheeled into Berlin's Olympic stadium which was adorned with flags—the red swastika was ubiquitous. En masse, officials and spectators saluted Hitler and his entourage. Coubertin spoke to 110,000 spectators and an overseas radio audience. He extolled the virtues of participation in the Games, code words that have been taken to mean to-be-the-best-that-one-can-be. His speech concluded with what can only be seen as a cosmic irony: "Just as in life, the aim is not to conquer, but to struggle well."

But the Berlin Games also told the story of American Jesse Owens, who won four gold medals. Much had been made of Owens' ethnicity, a black man who was understood to be less than human in his home country, and not worthy of the ideal of German superiority that Hitler had crafted.

Remarkably, Balke wrote in his autobiography, sixty years after the fact, that he had watched Owen's astounding gold medal performance in the 100 meters. He held Owen's athleticism in wonder, aware that he had won three other gold medals (200-meters, long jump and 4x100m relay). Balke's role as a spectator is a curiosity. As a student of Diem, indoctrinated with the ideals of Olympism, he had remembered the outstanding performances, a display of athleticism that had been imprinted on his memory banks. It was as if his education and experience of athleticism had transcended the politics of his day.

World War II began in September of 1939, three years and one month after the Opening Ceremonies of the Berlin Olympic Games. By then, Balke had completed his medical studies and had been a member of a mountaineering team that made a failed attempt to summit Nanga Parbat in the Himalayas. Along the way, he had escaped the ravages of an avalanche and somehow survived a lightning strike. He had also gotten married and welcomed a newborn son into the world and, when war came knocking, he was drafted into military service as a medical officer. By the spring of 1940 he found himself on the Western Front dodging gunfire.

Balke's autobiography, written in the latter years of his life, referred to an attitude he had come to adopt to describe his life's journey; he called it *'optimistic fatalism.'* He reasoned that this ideal gave meaning to all the horrors he had little control over. He endured. He believed because of optimistic fatalism, a belief born of the ideals of Olympism, that no matter what fate had in store, he had doubled down, disciplined his mind and his body, he had carried on.

'Optimistic fatalism,' in hindsight, seems like an idea that embraced Jesse Owens' courageous performances, Carl Diem's innovations, and Pierre de Coubertin's Olympic dreams. For me and my family, optimistic fatalism would overcome our doubts and fears, not the least of which was the fear of my crippledom. It was an ideal that my father would embrace, and

it fueled the early days of my athleticism. It served as a useful guidepost for our collective dream to build a better life after the suffering of the depression, the horrors of world wars, and the random taking of life by devastating disease.

My father wholeheartedly believed in optimistic fatalism; he called it common sense.

CHAPTER THREE

The Joy of Effortlessness (1991)

"If you follow your bliss, you put yourself on a kind of track that has been there all the while, waiting for you, and the life that you ought to be living is the one you are living. Wherever you are—if you are following your bliss, you are enjoying that refreshment, that life within you…"
Joseph Campbell and the Power of Myth with Bill Moyers

By my thirty-seventh year I had learned to live, almost exclusively inside the world of science, evidence-based facts. Science stories—numbers and words fitting together like a puzzle revealing a whole truth. And then there was my other story, a broken truth about my own Olympic dreams that I had buried deep inside, like the smallest of nesting dolls, out of sight, out of mind. Besides, the scandals and corruption of the Games that had erupted over my lifetime had been appalling. Was I not glad that I had never been a part of that?

My family was settling into a new home. It was several weeks after school had begun, and my two children, aged ten and eight, were tucked away at their desks, finishing their schoolwork. I had been stressed for most of that week and spent the morning mapping out a strategy for the week ahead. Transporting the kids from home to school, and from school to sports practices, while getting myself to and from work on time, was going to be impossible. We would be late, and I hated being late.

But what was worse was the prickly unease that had kept me from a good night's sleep, tossing and turning while ruminating over something as inconsequential as my son's fourth-grade football game.

Late August was when his football practices had started, and mothers took turns driving. One day, I had a van full of boys excited to wear genuine football gear, especially their brand-new purple football jerseys—the color of the Minnesota Vikings. As I drove, there was a flurry of body butts testing the strength of their equipment punctuated by nervous questions. Had I remembered the snacks? Did I know the coach? Was there a place to pee? Why did their refs not wear striped shirts like the TV refs?

But the prior week, the first football game of the season had taken me to a dark place. I had come directly from teaching physiotherapy students, and I was late. I hurried from the parking lot to the sideline of the football field. My dress shoes gathered up clumps of mud and fresh-cut globs of grass. I was still dressed in a navy blue suit while the other mothers wore jeans and sweatshirts, tennis shoes and baseball caps that held their ponytails. I was an outlier—a working mother. Loud, rude, sucking noises accompanied my every step as my shoes extracted themselves from the sinkholes of the wet field. I came to a stop a comfortable distance from the other parents.

Autumn had descended, and the trees that ringed the school playground were on the verge of bursting with color. In the middle of the field, the boys huddled and broke toward their assigned roles at the scrimmage line. My son crouched behind the quarterback, who grunted for the ball. On cue my son stutter-stepped, grabbed the ball, and began to run up the field.

Despite his oversized football gear, one arm cradled the ball, the other fell in sync with his stride as it stretched outward, gaining speed and length. His head steady, his body churning. I hoisted myself onto the balls of my feet, bobbing up and down to see past the line of parents. The tips of my shoes pressed deeply into the muddy grass. I leaned farther, shifting my weight onto my right leg, less on the left leg. Automatically I tilted my arms backward, chest forward, neck and head poking. My body balanced. Long ago a useful skill for the end of a close race, but now an unconscious balancing act that allowed me to watch my son. A touchdown, his first, a possibility.

I felt a swell of joy and pride that merged with the art of my lean. I may have yelled his name as if adding my breath would spur him into the end zone.

Out of nowhere, another voice struck a blow, knocking me back on my heels. Out of the corner of my eye, an arm covered by the sleeve of a business suit came into view, ramrod straight and attached to an angry fist with a bony index finger that sighted my son.

"Kill him! Kill him!" The arm tracked my son as he ran past tackler after tackler.

"Get him! Get Him!" The crack of a rifle seemed imminent.

My son ran faster, reached the end zone, dropped the ball, and threw up his hands, a touchdown gesture like the players he had seen on TV. The crowd fell into cheers and clapping, the mysterious arm disappeared, and the coaches of both teams called the boys together.

A purple group formed on one sideline, a green one on the other. Some boys were tall and lean, some short and thick, and others were goofy and awkward, but you could tell they loved to huddle like real football players. They were all from the same grade, school, and neighborhood.

I swallowed hard and extracted my shoes from the mud. Had the boys heard the call to violence? What were the coaches saying? A cool breeze washed my flushing face. I stopped my teeth from grinding and took in a breath to calm my pounding heartbeat. Too much drama. I forced a smile—there had been no gun.

"Ten-year-old's do not care who wins; they probably did not even hear what the parents were yelling," my husband said later that day. "Just kids having fun."

"Yeah, but still, I hate that win-at-all-costs attitude, and now obscene gestures. Especially in front of kids! What were these adults thinking?" I was venting.

We had just moved into this popular urban community, lured by its good school system. The price of the house had stretched our financial comfort zone, adding to a niggling sense of unease. Had this been a mistake? Was this a community where we could thrive?

I found no resolution after replaying the incident and decided to just let it go. After all, it was just kids playing a game. No big deal. Why let one overly ambitious guy, living his athletic dreams through his children, ruin my Sunday? It was my time to exercise. I had a favorite routine of running, walking, and jogging, that mocked my adolescent obsession of training to win races, to become an Olympian. Then I pushed my body to breathlessness, even though it hurt. Now, I just let my body do whatever it felt like. It never felt like working too hard.

I reached for my cassette player, fit my headset over my ears, and tucked the miniature recorder inside the pocket of my pink hoodie. I had an hour, possibly forty-five minutes before the family would make its demands: a football practice for my son, grocery shopping, and then reconfiguring the dinner hour to accommodate a random gymnastics lesson for my daughter.

She was fearless, and yet, as a physiotherapist, I worried about the aftermath of the punishing practices that the sport of gymnastics would put her body through. She loved the gym, but shamelessly I had been praising the virtues of soccer and her new baby blue t-shirt adorned with a ghostly soccer ball logo. Did she not *just love'* the color blue? Besides, selfishly, I liked that soccer practices were as predictable as my son's football practices. Never on Sundays.

As I stepped outside, I was greeted by my favorite kind of autumn day, cool crisp air along with a sunlit hint of warmth. I turned right at the end of the driveway and began a slow jog. I flipped the switch to the cassette player, and words came tumbling into my head. I had read Joseph Campbell's *The Hero With a Thousand Faces*, and was now listening to his interviews with journalist Bill Moyers. His stories about heroes rang true—I had read about Olympic heroes, had met Olympic heroes, had shared their Olympic dreams, and had followed their nuggets of wisdom on how to become an Olympian.

Campbell's analysis of stories and myths had unearthed a common thread—it felt like words and stories were universal and humane; it felt like common sense, the clarion call of my parents. As I listened to Campbell, I hoisted myself skyward onto the balls of my feet, harmonizing my breath to each stride, a meditation while moving. I probably jogged and ran for several miles, waiting to feel tired and then transitioned to jogging and walking, playful intervals switching between exertion, effort, and a relaxing stroll. Each interval contained exactly fifty steps.

There was, however, an unexpected glitch, I stopped suddenly causing my toes to jam against the toe box of my runners. Campbell was telling the story from his days as a college track and field athlete running the final leg of a relay. I knew he must have been a talented racer; coaches often assigned the fourth leg to the fastest sprinter on the team. He was behind the leader and passionately predicted that he would make up the distance between himself and his competitor. The voice from the recording paused, a silence that felt unbearable.

When he restarted, he spoke about the sound of his racing, his footfall hitting the track, and how he sensed that he could go faster. His feet did not touch the ground, to overtake the leader a possibility. He remembered gaining ground, and yet everything else was out of reach of his perceptive senses. His mind had dimmed while his body was overtaken by the kind of power that felt like absolute effortlessness.

Did he overcome the distance between himself and the other sprinter? Did he win? It seemed like this should be important, but I could only focus on his memory of effortlessness. '*My feet never touching the ground*,' he said, the same words I had said to myself after I ran a personal best in a 50-meter sprint, twenty years earlier.

I restarted my jog, counted my fifty steps, and then walked. My mind split in two: I had buried that sensation of effortlessness, categorized it as irrationally goofy, probably best explained by the theory of endorphins giving athletes a natural high, equivalent to hippiedom, a lighthearted lifestyle that I had never wanted to understand.

And now, Campbell's words erased that theory. It felt as if we shared the secret of effortlessness, and my effortlessness was as familiar as a long-lost friend.

I retrieved the cassette recorder from my pocket. Baby tears formed in the corner of my eye. Words stopped filling my head, and the recorder in my hand took on the aura of a halo—small, tiny rainbows embracing an absolute truth. It, effortlessness, was not an endorphin high; it was not frivolous, it was what had made me happy.

My toes wiggled free of my toe-box. Hoisting myself onto the balls of my feet, I felt the edge of effortlessness, a stance that had become my source of power and speed; a confident sense that I embodied as a high school track star. I was a sprinter who defied gravity. Some would call me a natural-born athlete.

Defying gravity had been my bliss, the life I thought I would be living, and yet, I had failed to live that life even when I had a chance to make my dreams come true. Should I not have done more to follow my bliss? Had it not been my destiny—a time when I knew who I was and where I was headed? All of it, the sensing, the thinking, and the doing, I had privileged it all, and it was all that mattered.

But I had failed because when I followed what I was passionate about, I discovered I needed to be better. I feared failure, and so I failed.

I wiped away the tears, turned the tape recorder over, and wiggled the connection between my headset and the metallic box. The buttons shaped like fingertips were stuck. The batteries had died.

I approached the kitchen door to my house meeting up with loud voices.

"Homework has to be finished before you go out to play!" my husband yelled.

My son opened the door and ran past me just as the words of my husband registered. Not doing your homework was a path to failure. From the corner of my eye, I could see my daughter who had changed into her pink leotard, practicing cartwheels on the back patio.

Without thinking, I sprung up onto the balls of my feet as my eyes flitted from his churning legs to her pointed toes, legs in flight.

I smiled despite my son's defiance of homework, my body electrified by the joy of my children, a never-ending surge of energy that I recognized as my own discovery of effortlessness. It was a perfect storm, a decisive moment; my thinking would have to embrace, from the ground up, the athleticism of my past, if I was to meet the challenges of the future, the what-ifs, the what-to-do next. Without another thought, I toe-walked my way into the kitchen.

CHAPTER FOUR

Holding onto the Ideals of Olympism: Optimistic Fatalism

"The Olympic flame was interpreted by all who saw it or read about it, or were told about it, as a symbol of a brighter future for which all the peoples of the world are yearning…"

Bill Collins

After WWII, those passionate about the Games saw a path from soldiering to a better life. I imagine this was the case for Bruno Balke, who ended the war living in Austria, and a young sprinter named Gerard Mach, the son of a German father and a Polish mother.

By 1949, Balke was on a US transport ship headed for San Antonio, Texas, a German scientist swept up by Operation Paperclip. He had spent the latter years of WWII, after recovering from a bout of infectious hepatitis, stationed at the Army Mountain Medical School in St. Johann (Tyrol), Austria. There he worked on projects to develop mountain rescue equipment and to establish research laboratories where he began to investigate the impact of the mountain environment on the human body, including performing risky experiments on himself and military pilots.

From 1950-1960, he worked first with US Air Force Aviation medicine, and then, from 1960-1964, for the Civil Aeromedical Research Institute of the Federal Aviation Administration. He performed experiments measuring the impact of environmental extremes on the cardiovascular system. Along the way, he developed equipment to measure the physiological responses of the human body, including the delivery of oxygen to working muscles, as research subjects were pushed to the point of exhaustion. He developed a protocol for fitness testing that is used to this day, and established exercise standards for patients with heart disease, professional athletes, and Olympians, as well as astronauts training to travel to the moon.

In the spring of 1964, Balke met with Dr. Leonard Larson, the head of the physiology department at the University of Wisconsin in Madison, who offered him an academic appointment. It was an opportunity to build a curriculum in exercise and environmental physiology leading to a PhD degree. Balke's vision was to develop an inside-out view of exercise, a program that he referred to as the study of bio-dynamics—a curriculum that appears to mirror the tenets of Coubertin's Olympism. There was to be discipline and motivation, an intellectual, academic translation of the no-pain-no-gain mantra.

During this time, he began to develop protocols to safely exercise heart patients, tweaking their intensity of training based on the responses of their blood pressure and heart rates to exercise as well as their symptoms. The patients were no longer on the road to becoming cardiac cripples, afraid to move from their bed or homes, and were now part of daily exercise training. The physical demands and discipline of daily exercise were encouraged. Gaining back a normal life was a patient's reward.

Through Balke, rehabilitation fitness had found a foothold. He even ventured into the realm of prevention establishing a fitness program for faculty members who he had found at high risk for cardiovascular disease. And then a local professional sports team came calling. He tested the Green Bay Packers and the Milwaukee Bucks, found they were grossly unfit, and then recommended training programs to improve their fitness for their sport.

When Balke emigrated to the US, Gerard Mach was fourteen years old. He grew up in Danzig, Poland, during WWII, exposed to the never-ending rounds of bombings as the city was invaded first by Germans then Russians. I imagine that he started his athletic career clearing soccer fields of rubble from bombs. A functional training exposing his body to a regime of activities that shaped endurance and strength. When the war years ended, he pursued first soccer and then athletics and became recognized as an elite player and provincial champion in the 100, 200, and 400-meters. In 1948, he left soccer for a career in track and field, and went on to win the first of his eleven national titles in the 400-meters.

With each subsequent Olympics that had resumed after the War, he pursued his dream to go for gold. As a 400-meter specialist, he won European championships and set national records. He was a self-taught athlete who gained a reputation as a tough competitor and a student of the sport. He was curious and a thinker who had ideas about training and sprinting that led to his success and yet contradicted the norms of the day. Mach's last Olympic competitions were in Helsinki at the 1952 Games. He faltered when he failed to make the finals in the 400- or 200-meters, but he was soon to begin another Olympic dream.

Prior to his races, the opening ceremonies had honored Paavo Nurmi, the Finn's national hero, by selecting him to light the Olympic flame. Mach probably watched as Nurmi entered the stadium noting his characteristic long stride, and approving of his soldierly posture, chest outward, ramrod straight as he reached to light the Olympic Flame. But still, Mach might also have had mixed feelings—admiration for Nurmi's accomplishments but also disdain over his training methods.

In Mach's opinion, Nurmi's philosophy of no-pain-no-gain while maybe okay for endurance athletes, was detrimental to an elite sprinter. Mach developed a coaching philosophy that steered away from what he saw as overtraining. He developed a set of functional exercises that facilitated power and speed with a relaxed effort. The precision of his coaching matched the biomechanical demands of the sprint. He once told me that the best sprinters attain top speed at sixty meters which they maintained until the finish, a precise finish—arms back, chest forward, head steady, a well-timed body lean.

Mach had a poetic flair, or maybe it was that Polish and German were his first languages. His English words were halting. But as my own career intersected with his coaching, I knew exactly what he meant. "To win," he would say and then smile, "to win, was to be the one who was the slowest to slow down."

To win was to move with grace, with effortlessness was what I thought I heard him say.

In my mind, the legacies of Balke and Mach, were shaped by the long arm of the past. In their own ways, they fostered an optimistic aura, no matter the vagaries of fate. Both probably had shuddered at the roar of airplanes and smelled the dusty stench of destruction, but were surefooted in their athleticism, disciplined and responsible. They were too busy to pay attention and so transcended politics. Both lived as any human being in the war years lived—they had dreamed of peace and as the war ended, they grabbed hold of the ideals of Olympism with a hardened determination to live their dream.

Mach would continue his career trusting his intuitive sense of athleticism grounded by his experience as an Olympic hopeful; Balke would continue his research as he wrote and rewrote the science story alongside his trusty slide ruler.

CHAPTER FIVE

Defying Gravity:
Thinking With Story

"Thinking with stories is a process in which we as thinkers
do not so much work on narrative as take the radical step
back, almost a return to childhood experience, of allowing
narrative to work on us."

David Morris, 2002

On the morning of July 20, 1969, I opened my eyes from
a fitful sleep—a fifteen-year-old girl anticipating my
first national track and field meet racing against athletes that
had come from all over Canada. Four days earlier, television
images of the lift-off of Apollo 11 had left me awestruck,
barely comprehending what I saw—a pencil-sharp cylinder
crawling skyward accompanied by a huge number—7.5 million
pounds—of thrust required for the spacecraft to defy gravity.

Winnipeg, my hometown, lies between two river systems,
the Red River, and the Assiniboine. The city was surrounded by
endless golden prairies, and was equidistant from Vancouver to
the west and Montreal to the east. My family had made several
attempts to take car trips to visit these larger historic places, but

had never made it, foiled by bad weather and lack of vacation time. Our driving force was nothing like rocket power, even when we only had to travel horizontal to the force of gravity.

On the edge of the city sat the Pan Am Stadium. A legacy facility with the fading logos of the 1967 Pan Am Games attached to fences and locker room walls. The blue-green artificial surface of the oval track was made-up of bits of rubber stuck to a springy surface. It had a faint smell of mold and for some unknown reason we called it a tartan track. Compared to the cinder and gravel surfaces we usually ran on; we believed this modern track would propel us to personal best times in our races. But even more so, the appearance of the Pan Am Games in our less than modern city, had fueled my Olympic dream—the thrill of victory injected with the excitement of travel to not only Montreal and Vancouver, but also, if I was good enough, to travel by airplane to international competitions in New Zealand, Jamaica, and my dad's favorite, Scotland. To travel by airplane, at the expense of the Canadian government, was an astonishing fact.

Meanwhile, the astronauts had reached the moon in record time and were beginning to complete detailed checklists in preparation for their evening moonwalk. After eating breakfast and laying out my running clothes, I only had to wait for the time to leave for the stadium. I plunged into my then favorite book—*Gone With the Wind*. I chose books by their titles, curious as to what exactly was gone and how the wind made it so. Instead, I found the romance of southern culture—velvet dresses ballooning outward, sweeping down grand staircases, while male suitors looked upward. I imagined elegance moving step-by-step in unison with gravity.

As I peered out my bedroom window, I saw the heat of the day come into view, a slow rising shimmer undeterred by the hope of a cool breeze. I delayed leaving the house. It was too hot to undergo my usual warm-up routine and I was eager to read just one more chapter. My father paced and fussed about the possibility of congested traffic, the uncertainty of finding a parking spot, and the importance of my doing well. And then, as we drove to the stadium track: Did I remember to bring my racing shoes? I corrected him. They are called Adidas racing shoes. Special white rubber-soled shoes with threaded holes where I could screw in one-quarter inch metal spikes— short thick barbs positioned where the ball of my foot struck the ground as I sprinted, the source of my effortlessness.

I am certain he asked me about my shoes because I was known for forgetting important things, but I cannot remember if we had to go back and get the shoes, or if I won or lost my races that day. What I do remember is that I failed to do my routine warm-up and that my competitors wore fancy, expensive running clothes and what appeared to be Adidas spikes as well as Puma's, another brand that we all thought was not as good as the Adidas.

The truth is that I probably lost my races. And what I felt about losing those races seemed unimportant on the day that

Neil Armstrong, an athletic man of science who had ridden the space capsule atop the unimaginable rocket power, had reached the moon and then walked on its surface. His footprints had been imprinted in the moon dust for the first time in history. Every time I gaze at the full moon and see its shadows, I wonder about the possibilities that they still can be found, large footprints dug deep into the moon dust, a permanent record just like the memory of that historic day.

Dinnertime that day was a mish mash of aching leg muscles and the excitement of the upcoming moonwalk that was to be shown on TV. I also remember the warm glow of a sunburn creeping up my face and across my shoulders. After dinner, I went to my bedroom and sank into the coolness of my bed covers. I fell into a whole-body sleep, but kept a part of my consciousness alert, anticipating the call from my mother for when it was time to watch the historic moonwalk.

My bedroom was dark when I heard her excited voice. It sounded far away calling me again and again. My eyes struggled to open completely, and the sunburnt skin of my arms slid across the soft fake fur of my pink poodle, a stuffed toy animal that had once soothed my itching from chicken pox. When I finally opened my eyes, the moon, full and bright, took up the space of the bedroom window, a full moon its surface marked with dark gray squiggly shadows. I imagined large footsteps slowly forming with the rise and fall of giant frosty-white boots. It was as if I was seeing the moonwalk through my bedroom window.

The next day, I watched Neil Armstrong as he descended the ladder and took his first step onto the surface of the moon. Over and over, the stepping replayed. There is both awkwardness and grace, a body floating and landing. Oversized moon-dusted footprints appeared accompanied by a silent footfall, and then hissing and beeping, words and breath coming and going with each step as the globed-head of the astronaut bobbed from side to side.

The story of nineteen-year-old John Gillespie Magee, a WWII spitfire pilot emerges. Although he was an American, he eagerly joined the war effort, after crossing into Canada to join the Royal Canadian air force. He wrote a poem to his parents shortly before his death in a mid-air collision over Lincolnshire England on Dec 11, 1941.

Oh! I have slipped the surly bonds of Earth
And danced the skies on laughter-silvered wings;
Sunward I've climbed, and joined the tumbling mirth
of sun-split clouds, — and done a hundred things
You have not dreamed of——wheeled and soared and swung
High in the sunlit silence. Hov'ring there,
I've chased the shouting wind along, and flung
My eager craft through footless halls of air....

American broadcasters read the poem many times accompanied by the swell of patriotic music as they declared themselves the winner of the race to the moon. The race was known to all. It was the battleground for the cold war in the aftermath of WWII. It was yet another race that Balke had been a part of, not physically, but because his science stories had played an integral part in preparing astronauts to endure the rigor of space travel. Reportedly millions of people watched the moonwalk, after following the years of progress that allowed space travel. It was as if the whole world had stopped paying attention to the details of their day-to-day lives and collectively felt the wonder of space travel, and then the absolute astonishment of the moon walk.

Collectively we heard the words of Neil Armstrong just before he stepped onto the moon: '*One small step for man, one giant leap for mankind.*' McGee's words may also have hovered: wheeling, soaring, swinging, chasing a universal awakening about the humanness of defying gravity. It was a first for all of mankind, to dream of walking on the moon, to use rocket power to travel to a far-off place, and to make our dreams come true.

And just like the lost memory of my races that day, I wonder if the fact that the US had won the race to the moon is also lost. The memory of the moon walk—a small step and then a giant leap fused with soaring, wheeling, and '*slipping the surly bonds of earth, of doing a hundred things we could not dream,*' evoked humanity's gasp of cosmic wonder. Defying gravity was what we felt and saw, it had an emotional valence, and it mattered more than we could ever know.

Defeating gravity by rational thought was also underway in my hometown in 1969. Dr. David Winter had recently been appointed the director of biomedical engineering at the Shriner's Hospital—an institution immersed in the rapidly growing field of medical rehabilitation. His life's work merged the evolving advances in technology to his knowledge of Newtonian forces—using the power of numbers to understand human movement—a pathway to solving physical disability. An urgent quest. Winnipeg had been an epicenter for the polio epidemics of the 1950s. The aftermath of this illness impacted how young people moved, attended school, went to work, built a life. Many survivors now faced a lifetime of getting around on limbs that would not support their bodies.

To reduce the complexity of the problem, he drew stick figures. Lines drawn to represent parts of the body, dots representing joints all topped off with a head drawn as a circle, with no eyes, just a nose that pointed the stick figure in the direction for an imaginary walk. As he molded technology to fit his scientific quests, direction of forces, angles of joint movement, notations for joint velocities, and then instantaneous accelerations appeared on his figures. Underneath these drawings his words conjured an image that summed it all up, both literally and metaphorically—defying gravity was like the movement of an inverse pendulum—a body vaulting over its feet.

Forty-six years later, remnants of Winter's work can be found in the myriad of video games that mimic the actions of professional athletes. Powerful computers and their binary imagination produce these animations. But if you look closely the movement of the avatars is a bit off, an awkward subtle tick-tocking accompanies each step.

If Dr. Winter were alive, would he frown? The computing of the numbers associated with the stick figures produced walking that mimics the inverse pendulum of a grandfather's clock, swaying over fixed feet accompanied by the sound of tick-tocking. Time along with energy passing away.

Later, when I was in university, when the astonishment of the moonwalk was long forgotten, I remember struggling to understand Winter's numbers that produced the inverse pendulum. I had never taken calculus, and had been frustrated by high school physics. I began to write myself a new story: tick-tocking to defy gravity had been a wondrous idea, it looked like the moonwalk, and yet there was something that did not make sense, not quite right. The sense of the inverse pendulum, a tick-tocking that looked effortless, had never been my idea of defying gravity. My power grew from the ground up. Toe-walking was effortless because I pushed-off releasing the accumulated power of my leg thrusting my body forward.

Never sideways.

We lived in a three-bedroom, one bathroom house. A narrow hallway separated me and my sister's bedroom from that of my parents. My bed shared the wall with the hallway while my sister's bed was under the window on the outside wall of the house. My mother once told me that the night before I raced, she would be awakened by my knees bumping and pounding against the wall.

I remember those dreams. They would start with cheering crowds and wind blowing, and then the tap, tap, tap of my racing shoes hitting the pebbled surface of the track. I'm running the 200-meters, hugging the inside of my lane at the Pan Am Stadium. I enter the turn, having already successfully caught up to the runners in the outside lanes.

I enter the last part of the turn and suddenly, a cool shadow passes overhead. I feel it on the back of my legs and goosebumps ratchet up the hair on the back of my neck. I feel their ache. More, do more, I tell myself, lift your thighs, faster, go faster.

The cheering fades away, replaced by a thunderous rumble. The pace of the dream slows. A force grabs my shirt and pulls me backwards. I pump my arms and legs only to discover that I am now going nowhere, forever stuck at the end of the turn unable to push-off.

I'm tick-tocking, swaying side to side, almost standing still and running out of energy.

Thudding followed by a bruising pain. My eyes pop open and I stop my knees from hitting the wall, shocked by the tick tocking and my loss of power. I wiggle my toes as they dig into the coolness of my bed covers and the old joy of effortlessness seeps to the surface.

Scientists tell us that our brains manufacture nightmares so as to work out the stresses of daily life. Scraps of memories and thought being reshaped to fit the narratives that we tell ourselves. Neuroscientists have even located exactly where these stories live. Indeed, it is not on the brain's surface, but underneath billions of neurons folded over on themselves sending out tiny threads that weave a web as the vital, dream-forming connections develop.

My fear of losing and the joy of effortlessness played out as dream stories. An exhausting noisy, bruising battle fighting against an awkward tick-tocking as my mind frantically searched for the power of the push-off.

An endless battle over fear, sometimes disguised as a globe-headed astronaut—a story that tick-tocked its way into my gravity-defying dreams, always on the night before a race.

CHAPTER SIX

Dueling Narratives: A Matter of Priorities

"…Coubertin's best-known aphorism… is really a quote from the bishop of Pennsylvania…the important thing in these Olympiads is *less* to win than to take part in them."

Sigmund Loland

Coubertin believed wholeheartedly that sport mattered, but he wavered in his belief of the importance of winning. In his memoirs of 1908, he described sport as an endeavor that would enrich the lives of the individual. Through the display of athletic dramas, all individuals would learn and be inspired by the spectacle of athleticism to take up sport as a means to achieve high moral character. To participate on a global stage embraced the nobility of sport. The being-the-best-you-can-be narrative aligned itself with Coubertin's often-quoted ideal that to win was less important than to take part.

In his memoirs of 1931 however, he was also adamant that the record of athletic performance symbolizes '*the summit of the sport edifice.*' Winning was paramount. Striving to be the best in the world was the motivation that inspired athletes to dedicate themselves to spell-binding performances. '*Swifter,*

Higher, Stronger,' became the shorthand for those who climbed to the top, achieving world and Olympic records. Participation became the clarion call of athletes who came in second, or worse, had no chance of winning a medal.

The ambivalence of Coubertin's vision on how Olympism embraced winning was battered about by nationalism and politics and the desire of athletes to win at all costs. And to his credit it may have been a factor in Coubertin's resignation from the IOC in 1925. Bruce Kidd, in his essay *A New Orientation to the Olympic Games*, wrote that when Coubertin saw that the IOC *'...was neglecting its mission of education and reflection and devoting nearly all its time to the technical side of the Games,'* he resigned from the presidency. In Canada, it appeared that there was another chapter to add to the dueling narratives, and Bruce Kidd was taking up the challenge to reconcile the contradictions.

Kidd's inspiration started brewing with the track and field competitions of the 1952 Helsinki Games, which brought together a changing of the guard between those athletes who were scarred by the war, who were determined to build a better life for themselves, and those who had been born after the war. Paavo Nurmi, the Flying Fin, met and befriended an Australian by the name of John Landy, a young middle-distance runner who was rumored to be on the verge of running a sub-four-minute mile, which he did at an international meet in Vancouver, Canada, in 1954. Although beaten by Roger Bannister, they had both broken the four-minute record. A statue honoring the moment of the race's final steps, sculpted by Jack Harman, was re-dedicated in 2015 at the Empire Stadium in Vancouver, the place where the race was run almost sixty years earlier.

Landy's race in Vancouver against Bannister was nicknamed the Miracle Mile. A race watched by a young Bruce Kidd, who went on to a remarkable career as a Canadian hopeful in distance running. According to Bruce Kidd, even though Landy had lost, he was a meaningful inspiration for his athletic career.

Landy was also known for his performance at the Australian National Championships prior to the Melbourne Games of 1956. At the halfway mark of the mile, Landy's fellow competitor, Ron Clark, was accidentally tripped. Landy clipped Clark while trying to avoid running into him. Several strides later, he turned back, helped Clark to his feet and finished the final two laps, coming in first. A display of sportsmanship embraced by excellence.

In the 1960s, as Kidd prepared for international competitions, the ideology of excellence, to win-at-all-costs, was gaining momentum forged by the no-pain-no-gain philosophies of Nurmi. For Kidd this had resulted in leg and foot injuries and competitive fatigue, which took their toll. At the 1964 Tokyo Games, he failed to make the finals in the 5000-meters and placed 26th in the 10000 meters. His fellow competitors were shocked. They encouraged him to bounce back, redouble his efforts to win. Later, he would write of the devastation he felt and the public humiliation by the Canadian press, but also the '*international competitive fellowship*' he had experienced. He wrote about the common bond between competitors born of the no-pain-no-gain philosophy that they had all endured. Years later, as I read his account, a spark of an idea began to take shape. Winning or losing, when all was said and done, was about being-the-best-you-can-be and not a single-minded pursuit of excellence. What I wanted to believe, what I hoped that Kidd was telling me: being-the-best-you-can-be was not just for athletes who failed.

The story of Bruce Kidd was also rooted in the joy of movement. He had a flowing, unusual running style, which according to his memoir, began as a young child, bouncing off the walls of a New York apartment where he lived part of his childhood. His abilities were recognized as a school athlete, and his career was launched. His finishing kicks were a thrill for spectators to watch. During the heady days of becoming the darling of Canadian middle distance running, the call came to be featured in a documentary which was released by the Canadian National Film Board in 1962.

Producer Don Owen wanted the documentary to adhere to the spirit of the ancient Greek Games. He enlisted the poet W.

H. Auden to write the script. At one time in his career, Auden worked to emulate the poetics of the classical Greek poet Pindar, who had extolled the virtues of the victorious Greek Olympians. It was fate, a moment where a talented athlete was in the right place at the right time, infused with the poetics of ancient Greece. Surely, Coubertin would have been overjoyed to see how olympism and athleticism embraced artistry, bringing to life his deep conviction that sport mattered.

The eleven-minute documentary starts with Kidd running along Lake Ontario, birds chirping, waves washing the shore underneath the boardwalk, and the rhythmic tapping of Kidd's footfall. A perfectly calm body connecting to the artistry of Auden's words.

Trees, grasses, children's voices, and cyclists come into view adding to the slow tick tock of a double bass in sync with Kidd's footfall. A soft drumbeat follows and then a crisp snap of a snare. The music gains volume.

The narrator tells of Kidd's dedication to his schedule of training: two hours a day, six days a week, an average of a hundred miles. The music gains speed and more volume as we watch a headless crowd of legs churning, keeping pace with the beat. Trumpets arrive along with other athletes, sprinters, relay runners, and the face of a coach holding a stopwatch as well as an official firing a pistol to signal the start of a sprint.

The camera's view resonates with the jazzy riff as the focus turns to Kidd's running style. His face relaxed and floppy, his arms circling, the outside of his forefoot hits the cinder track and rolls, the heel briefly lowers and then hoists his body forward. The narrator theorizes that there is balance, and grace that *'the limbs learn to live the movement.'*

I see absolute effortlessness.

A dozen runners prepare to advance to the starting line of a two-mile race. Among them are Bruce Kidd and Hungarian Lazlo Tabori, who had defected to the US, fleeing the Soviet takeover of his country after Tabori had competed in the 1956 Melbourne Games. He learned English while working as a janitor, and then, with his engineering background, went on to design wheelchairs for the disabled, and start his own business selling running shoes. After retiring from running, he coached recreational and elite athletes, at clubs, schools, and universities, as well as women Olympians and world record holders in the New York and Boston City marathons. But on that sunny day in Canada, with the cameras poised, he was the underdog to the Canadians' favored son.

The documentary falls silent as the runners line up. The starter's pistol fires into the air. The line of runners leaps forward.

The trumpets are blaring, the sounds of the crowds cheering and clapping as the laps are run. Near the end of the race, Kidd takes the lead and never looks back, well, maybe just once. He crosses the finish line as the winner. The crowd cheers and Kidd immediately sits on the ground and unties his shoes. In his memoir, Kidd writes that he often suffered foot blisters, so it makes sense that he is quick to take his shoes off to find relief from the the well-worn skin, ripped open by the hundreds of footfalls.

I like to think that in winning this race, Kidd felt the poetry, not just the pain of his blisters. Had joy and relief overcome the temporary soreness?

The documentary is a brilliant artistic accomplishment, poetry in motion. Kidd and Tabori merge with Nurmi, Landy, Coubertin, Pindar, and Auden. Taken together they tell an epic story that moves, creating an aesthetic link centered on the joy and beauty of movement, that forges the bond between past and present. Winning was decidedly not the priority.

Kidd ended his athletic career soon after the 1964 Games, completed his education and then began to work in government, and then went on to academic positions at the University of Toronto. His memoir documents his pursuit of gathering 'critical evidence' to support the impact of sport on individuals and communities. He was on the hunt for facts, but he also collected stories of other athletes who had also felt the impact of the dueling narratives. The quest would be complicated. As an athlete, he had nurtured his joy of running, dedicated himself to the grand ideals of sport, unearthed the bond of competitive fellowship and suffered the humiliation of his failure to win.

He would spend the rest of his career attempting to keep the climb to the '*summit of the sport edifice*' from overwhelming the joy, beauty, and grace of the '*story that moves...'*

CHAPTER SEVEN

Discovering Common Sense

"...life histories become coherent and credible
only by invention, often in defiance of known fact."

David Lowenthal

When I was in the ninth grade I attended St Mary's Academy, an all-girls school loosely concerned with paving the way for girls to become nuns. I sat in the very back row of the classroom. My desk was closest to the doorway that led to a long hallway. Individual music rooms, each one topped by a stained-glass transom that levered outward, lined the opposite side of the hallway to my classroom. This was the old part of the school, and it smelled like dirty socks and dried wood, and was always devoid of sunlight.

Throughout the day students came to the music rooms and practiced piano or took a music lesson. Muffled words, often stern and screechy and punctuated by the slap of a ruler across knuckles, seeped into my classroom. The music soared, mingled with the crack of the ruler and absent cries of pain. I wondered how this could be allowed. This was the 1970s. Corporal punishment had been banned. But I was listening through walls. Everything muffled, like my body draped in a dull-colored blue uniform while my mind split in two.

Rows of desks spread out before me. Sister Catherine, tall and old and puffy, sat at the head of the classroom. Her face pinched by a black and white headdress. Once, as I turned in some worksheets, I accidentally touched the back of her hand. My fingers sank into its crinkly white skin and left an indentation the size of my fingertip. She had taught my father when he was my age, and everyone thought this was a grand connection, past to the present, except me and Sister Catherine. I spent the year fearful I would do something wrong, one of those wrongs that I had no knowledge of; she would have been eager to tell my father.

She taught us British history, speaking from memory. She turned the pages of our history book as she spoke, but never looked down at the words. And then there was algebra. Balancing equations, when she would call us up in rows to the chalkboard so everyone could see our work. "2x times (3x +4) equals 20. Solve for x."

I loved the feel of the chalk as the numbers danced in front of my eyes. I knew how to find the elusive x and I bounced up and down onto the balls of my feet. Words, books, and chalk intermingled with scales and the strains of classical music, Beethoven's "Für Elise" a favorite piece, music that went from a slow and peaceful jog to a fevered race embracing a distant thwack and my looming springtime exams.

Some days, science books, along with musty smells, yellowed pages, and frail book bindings, replaced her history orations. Pictures made from wood cuts appeared on almost every page alongside words of awe and wonder. Science was a mystery that had yet to be solved. Airplanes, the book revealed, on the verge of becoming a reality just as the roar of an airplane blew into the classroom through an open window. Sister Catherine believed wholeheartedly in fresh air, as she expounded on the future that the airplane would bring. Not one student flinched, but we all knew she had not heard what we knew to be already a fact of the modern world.

Just outside the classroom door was a metal fire door that led to the new part of the school. Opening the door, always resulted in a temporary blindness due to the floor to ceiling windows that lined the hallway. In the modern part of the school was a beautiful theater, with tiered seating that formed a gently curbing semi-circle around a large stage framed by a thick, red velvet curtain, which rose and fell on everything public in our school: choir and piano recitals, plays, even an opera, also popular local musicians, speakers, the first-day-of-school reunions, and graduation farewells. We sat in plush seats. Sometimes I would slip my feet from my school shoes and sink them into the thick, crimson red carpet.

I felt safe in the theater, and the modernity that echoed as our shoes click-clacked over the hallway's stone floors. The new part of the school also held a brand-new gymnasium and student science laboratories. About once a week we attended gym classes, and with an inescapable irony, learned how to do experiments in the science labs. Despite the airplane debacle, we sat at benches and learned what a science experiment was, how to follow the steps, observe its outcomes, and how to document our results in coil-bound laboratory manuals.

Sister Joanne was our gym teacher. Every week she pinned up her long black skirts, pulled her head veil back into a knot and donned her bright white running shoes. We exchanged our heavy blue uniforms with white shorts, runners, and socks, topped off by blue blouses. We played volleyball, a lot, and getting the ball over the net was an all-consuming challenge. We also had a full basketball court. She coached me to get to the ball and give it to Theresa who could curl up towards the net and score a basket. We played other all-girls schools and lost by large margins.

The gym was also where we practiced sprinting out of starting blocks, high jumping, and shot put. In the springtime, we went outside onto the school grounds, a grassy, treed space that had jumping pits and a road where we could run. Springtime also brought an onslaught of exams, as well as time devoted to practicing for a school track meet run by the Knights of Columbus. We had a part-time coach, Mr. Lucas, a former sprinter, who had competed against a famous Canadian athlete named Harry Jerome.

Mr. Lucas told us stories about his races against Jerome, a Canadian hero who had at one time held the world record for the 100-meters. They had run on a black cinder track at the University of Saskatoon. Within two years, I would be at the same starting line, running in a Tri-Provincial track meet, reading the plaque that heralded Jerome's world record accomplishment. My race was a disaster. I had leaned for the finish line and fell, skinning my right knee and thigh, losing the race, and collecting an impressive amount of tiny black cinders deeply embedded in my skin. First aid was applied and unbeknownst to me, I was allergic to the Elastoplast bandages. I arrived home, with my thigh covered in hives that had coalesced into crusty weepy islands of black cinders, moated by a fiery red inflammation. Exhausted, I fell into bed with my leg free from the covers, ramrod straight, only to be woken in the dark of night by my parents hovering over my leg, shocked at its sight—demanding to know exactly what had happened.

Mr. Lucas never talked about the art of the lean, meaning one where you did not fall. But he patiently taught the importance of 'warming up' including stretching exercises, carefully paced wind sprints, each activity attached to numbers and an attention to how our bodies responded. We never were excused from the warm-up—it was how we readied our bodies to run. I could tell Mr. Lucas was an expert. In my mind, he, and Harry Jerome, the first Black men I had known, were physical educators, and I was eager to learn and to perform. Sister Catherine's history and the new science were secondary—more thinking than doing.

At the end of the school year, we competed as an all-girls team in the Knights of Columbus city-wide school track meet. My body ached with fatigue and my muscles were sore, and after races there were holes in my shoes where the ball of my foot had touched the ground. Sister Joanne watched over us at the meet and told me that I ran like a gazelle. She loved to watch me run and in a rush of excitement as we ended the track meet giddy and happy, filling up on water that Sister Joanne had arranged for, Mr. Lucas wondered out loud if the Olympics were in our future.

Over the next year, I attended other track meets with the help of Mr. Lucas. Expectations that I would someday be like the older more accomplished sprinters filtered into my brain. I discovered the world of club teams, one coached by a teacher from a local public school called the Galaxy Track Club. It wasn't long before I became convinced that I had to somehow prove to my parents that I should leave the nunnery.

Both my parents were Catholic, a common ground between my father's British and my mother's French heritages, despite a Canadian history fought by their ancestors over the cultural rule of English Canada and its British traditions, and the sidelining of French culture including their fiery expressive language. My parents were committed to providing us with a religious education, mostly rooted in Latin, that bound us to relatives and family tradition that often co-existed no matter what language was spoken. They had volunteered most of their free time when I was a child to raise money for the building of our local church and school, and had made many sacrifices to pay for private school for me, my sister, and brother. Neither of

my parents had gone to university, and in her teenage years, my
mother quit high school to work after her father died of a heart
attack.

Growing up I believed that we were the good guys in the
big scheme of things. Canadians won the war, single handedly,
according to my father who bolstered his claims with stories
of Lester B. Pearson, a jolly-looking man, short like my dad,
a Canadian hero who had received the Nobel Peace Prize.
Pearson's leadership had something to do with my brother
not having to go to war in a country named Israel, and me not
having to worry about nuclear bombs and hiding under my
desk. And my mother was adamant that we all get the polio
vaccine, a disease that was the scourge of her childhood. Tears
filled her eyes the day we lined up to take the sugar cube
with pink medicine knowing that we had been saved from
polio. Politics, science stories, and the miracles of medicine
dominated our dinnertime conversations. I was the most cared-
for person in the world.

The day finally came to talk with my parents. I cannot
remember where we were when we had the big discussion.
In the car? At dinnertime? In the downstairs family room that
my father had built?—everything with an orange hue that
resonated with the wildlife pictures by the environmentalist and
Manitoba artist, Clarence Tillenius. My father was a manager
of a small successful printing firm. I remember how he looked
at the Tillenius paintings. A thoughtful survey narrated by his
eye for color. My mother had told us that my father had the

gift of an artist. As a young man, he had worked his way up the ladder of the printing firm, first as a photographer shooting black and white and then color. He always had a camera on family vacations, and then a movie camera taking shaky 16mm film of my races. I remember he always had the smell of ink.

My father had built a bar in our downstairs family room. It was tiled with left-over navy blue book covers he brought home from his work. Behind the bar he had made a display of my medals and trophies that sat inside old picture frames he had nailed to the wall. I imagine that we probably sat in our orange family room, my words rising and falling amongst the artifacts of my successes.

My words: Glenlawn Collegiate home to the Galaxy Track Club. Better for training; an oval cinder track right outside their doors with aluminum stands for spectators. My music teacher lived nearby. I had by now taken piano lessons for ten years, so I would not have to give that up. Less of a transportation issue for my father who had to drive me to St. Mary's before he went on to work. I could walk to Glenlawn Collegiate.

I hit a nerve when I told them about the airplane debacle. Both my parents were curious, which had been a major motivation for our family summer vacations spent car camping as we visited provincial parks, the Rocky Mountains, and the Great Lakes. It was why as a family we had dreamed of the big cities—Vancouver or Montreal—destinations that our car trips had failed to achieve.

I also knew my parents had strong opinions about public schools; they were devoid of discipline, had bad influences, LSD, and marijuana—they could ruin a life. But I also knew that my parents believed in science. Besides, I was a '*good student*,' with good grades, practiced my piano, and I won races. I laid my science book flat, and showed them the page that stated that airplanes had not been invented. I may also have mentioned that the airplane would have gotten us to Montreal or Vancouver within hours, not days. It sealed the deal.

My words made sense as I spoke: rumors, doubt, probably fear too, had been met with the power of curiosity. Changing schools aligned with Lester Pearson, the polio vaccine, and their bet that I was a good student. We had found common ground and had not, according to my father's way of thinking '*gotten carried away.*' I remembered feeling giddy, after all it was not only common sense, but good sense. Together we had found some good sense, had we not?

And so, for the last three years of high school, we congratulated ourselves. I had found a love for chemistry taught by a master educator, Mr. Mutter. My English teacher, who looked like a character from a Shakespearean novel, would lead us into the world of tragedy and drama. I wrote a short story for a writing competition and came in third. My parents and I attended a community dinner in a hotel's dining hall filled with unathletic authors that seemed happy about the story I had written. My parents were happy. We basked in the good fortune of our good sense.

In public school, I found like-minded track friends. All of us trained and pushed ourselves, competing passionately, winning sometimes, losing too, but united by the pain of endurance runs, the stories of our athletic heroes, by physical injuries that would cause an absence from the team, and by a school spirit that we seemed responsible for. I found a close friend, a hurdler, who had a way of keeping my competitive big-headedness in check when I dismissed her feelings or best efforts. It was a lesson that I needed to learn again and again.

But life outside the nunnery, in this public place, did justice to the rumors, the facts of life that my parents feared. I was to learn that common sense and good sense did not always apply, that there was a breathless chaos, unpredictable moments that contradicted everything I or my parents believed in. There were no words that could explain the chaos I encountered. The safe way would be to keep the chaos at bay, disguised, brushed off, cleverly hidden from dinnertime conversations.

CHAPTER EIGHT

The Art of the Lean

"The will to do, the soul to dare."
Sir Walter Scott

The Games of Seoul, Korea, began on the seventeenth of September, 1988, and ended on the second of October, the events of which were a devastating blow to Olympism. But sometime in the same year, a small crowd gathered at Hallelujah Point along the sea wall in Vancouver's Stanley Park to dedicate a bronze statue of the Olympian Harry Jerome. The 9-foot effigy commemorated Jerome's running career as a sprinter. He had recently been declared the athlete of the century (1871-1971).

By all accounts, Jerome was a natural born athlete, a sprinter, born to a family of former Olympians. A standard bearer of athletic heroism, with no mention of a history of toe-walking, which to me, seemed as if somebody had omitted a vital chapter of his life. After all, the statue was and is a perfect balance of an athletic body powered by the toe-walking posture of his right foot.

The year 1988 yoked him to the Seoul Games and the disgrace of Canadian sprinter Ben Johnson. But unlike

Johnson, who won in Seoul leading by two strides, Jerome won his races because of his well-timed body lean, a feature of his races immortalized by the statue.

The sculpture miraculously leans perilously close to losing its balance, depicting a whole-body lean, arms flung backward, his chest crossing an imaginary finish line. His face is calm, his head steady, his eyes gazing at some point far along the path. His right thigh, mid-swing prepared for the next step. The power and balance, the largess of the statue, all of it defied gravity.

Many photographers have taken its picture during the light of day or as the sun sets, with the skyscrapers of Vancouver in the background. Not far from the statue is a bench that gives a side view of the statue. I have only been to Stanley Park once. I do not remember visiting the statue, but if I did see it, I would have sat on the bench for a long time to study this man. Gerard Mach, who coached the women's national sprint team before the Montreal Games in 1976 would have approved. The statue depicted a powerful lean, not one part of the sprinting form out of place.

Growing up I knew of Jerome. A national hero who had at one time carried the tag line as the fastest man on earth. He had come to Winnipeg to compete in the 1967 Pan Am Games, and had miraculously won the 100-meter gold medal by the slim margin conjured by his mighty lean. Journalists proudly wrote about his amazing comeback from a serious injury—*'the comeback of the twentieth century.'* But my family and I were oblivious. We had gotten free tickets to attend the equestrian events. Our dinnertime discussions centered on the athleticism of the horse and rider as they worked in concert to soar over wooden standards that were as tall as I was.

Jerome's talent emerged at the age of 18, after he broke the Canadian record in the 220-yard sprint held by the 1928 gold medalist, Percy Williams. Growing up, he excelled at a number of sports, but had chosen to train as a sprinter, over baseball and football. A choice, his sister would later recall, was due to the racist attitudes towards their family. He would be a three-time Olympian winning the bronze medal in the 100-meters at the 1964 Tokyo Games, and gold medals at the 1966 Perth Commonwealth Games and the 1967 Pan Am Games. Videos of those races would have caught his lean at the finish line, probably the same videos that inspired sculpturist Jack Harman's bronze statue, and in 2019, Toronto artist Moya Garrison-Msingwana's Google Doodle.

The posterior view of the statue exposed his lower right leg, his forefoot pushing off, his gastrocnemius muscle bulging. Thick, ropey edges define the hamstring muscles of both legs. Not a hint of which one had been injured. At the 1960 Games in Rome, he had severely torn his right hamstring and had not finished the race. Upon his return home, Olympic fans were devastated by his not winning. They called him a quitter.

And then another, more severe injury at the 1962 Commonwealth Games in Perth. In the final of the 100-meters, he severely tore his left quadriceps and did not finish the race. Perth physicians diagnosed a complete tear of his rectus femoris muscle, and upon his return to Canada, he underwent surgery. This time journalists declared that the rupture of a muscle tendon would be a career ending injury for an elite athlete, especially one that had failed, not once, but twice, to bring home the gold medal.

Dr. Hector Gillespie, an orthopedic surgeon who attended to the British Columbia Lions, a professional football team, operated on his leg soon after Jerome returned from Perth. During the surgery, Gillespie sutured muscle to tendon and then reattached the tendon to the connective tissue of the bone. For three months Jerome's leg was immobilized by a long leg cast. When it was removed, his quadriceps muscles would have been atrophied and flabby. He would have been able to feel the bumpy join between muscle, tendon, and bone as his hand massaged the healing incisions.

Reportedly, at the moment the muscle ruptured about halfway through the sprint, Jerome felt only a loss of power and not pain. I imagine that as he contemplated returning to competition, encouraged by Gillespie, and as his rehabilitation progressed, Jerome must have relived the moment when the muscle ruptured. His surgeon took a daring stance and enthusiastically encouraged Jerome to return to competition. Carefully titrated stretching exercises overcame the muscle pain and stiffness. Training sessions included prolonged warm-ups and carefully paced wind sprints followed by massages.

The pull and tug of healing tissues would erase the memory of the moment the injury occurred.

It is possible that as Jerome progressed from walking to jogging to running, he began to forget the moment in his races when the muscle tore. Strength and then power returned. Confidence grew. Within a year of his injury, he was again racing to the absolute amazement of everyone. Within a year of his injury, he had run a world record in the 60-meter dash at an indoor meet in Oregon.

Jerome retired in 1968 and went on to complete a master's degree in physical education. In his short life, he would teach and coach young athletes, building communities that would encourage participation in sport by organizing sporting events that was inclusive of recreational and elite athletes. He would lend his expertise in educating coaches and athletes and inspiring demonstration projects. He visited several of the first nations' reserves in the province of BC. No one was to be excluded.

Jerome's greatest legacy, according to his family, was not his athletic achievements now honored by track meets and community buildings named after him, but rather the fact that more than one million children received merit badges under his award programs. Harry Jerome was a student, an athlete, and a physical educator. He lived with racism and had overcome painful injuries. He was the epitome of the agony of defeat and the thrill of victory.

My parents would have talked about him in the same breath as their favorite politician, Lester B. Pearson, and they would have been proud that I had run on the same track where Jerome had set a world record, retelling the story of my race, the fall and the presence of the black cinders still embedded above my knee.

Although I never saw him run in person, his story and mine, through the happenstance of time, found common ground on that track in Saskatoon. For Jerome, the lean had won him many races, had shaved off the tenths of a second that resulted in world records. To become the fastest human on earth. It was part of his artistry, and the lean, so artfully depicted by the statue of Stanley Park, would also shape my future as an Olympic hopeful.

The statue was dedicated to honor his short life. In 1982, the year my son turned one year of age, Jerome collapsed and died of a ruptured cerebral aneurysm. He was only 42 years old.

CHAPTER NINE

The Lightning Strike

"Look into nature, and then you will
understand everything better."
Albert Einstein

Thunderstorms had always captured my curiosity. As a
young girl, especially on family camping trips when we
slept in a tent, they frightened me until my father taught me to
start counting when I saw a flash of lightning, and to stop at the
sound of thunder. A measure of how far away we were from the
danger of being struck by lightning.

After several years of tent camping, my mother declared
that she would no longer sleep on the ground. So, they rented
a camper trailer. It had a floor of hard wooden boards where
we slept, walls made of canvas and a roof made of aluminum.
My father declared that hauling a trailer across Canada was
impossible. Instead, he planned a three-week stay at a modern
campground at Riding Mountain National Park—about a two-
hour drive from where we lived. I envisioned swimming in the
pristine lake. I hoped we would see bears (the park was known
to be a place where they roamed) and continue with nightly

campfire rituals alongside swarms of fireflies, guitar music, and the roasting of marshmallows. None of it happened. Just days of rain, sitting in the camp shelter, wearing the only pair of green pants I had packed, playing board games until my fingers wore out and I lost the dice.

But there was one day and night that seared itself into my memory.

That day a caravan of cars pulled into a nearby campsite. Young, athletic-looking adults emerged and set up their tents in the rain. After dinner, as everyone huddled by a wood stove in the shelter, they arrived with Coleman lanterns that hissed and burned, converting fresh air into a sweet thick fog. At a nearby table, they unfolded maps, laughed, talked in serious tones, and pointed at the squiggles of road, drawing with their index fingers what appeared to be a never-ending journey. I was dying of curiosity. And I guess, so was my dad, because he finally went over to their table, and I followed him. We asked a lot of questions.

They were on a two-month vacation, teachers determined to reach Alaska. Their route would take them from Riding Mountain to Dawson Creek in northern British Columbia to meet up with the Alaskan Highway, a 1700-mile barely usable road plagued by steep grades, and switchbacks with few guardrails despite the steep hillsides. Frost heave might make some roads impassable, but they were counting on the summertime heat to melt the permafrost. They would camp wherever they found water and had carefully stored spare tires in case of a flat tire. I decided that these were not only campers but true adventurers.

As we walked back to our camper, my dad gushed with admiration for the teachers: the luxury of an eight-week vacation (he was only allowed three); the precision of their preparedness (he was certain they had thought of everything), and above all else they were fearless. Rain began to fall harder than before, and lightning flashed. We counted out loud. The storm was ten miles away. I felt the power of common sense. Being prepared and the solace of the number ten merged into one thought—to not be afraid felt good.

That night as I lay in bed, the rain pummeled the roof of the trailer, and thunder echoed. My mother was thankful that indeed we were off the cold wet ground. I feared for the teachers at first, in their flimsy looking tents, but then decided that for sure they would not leave tomorrow as they had planned—too rainy to travel—and hoped that I would be able to ask more questions. They had mentioned in passing that the year before they had traveled to South America. Their car trips ended at their planned destinations, something my family had failed to do.

A warming sun hit my face before my eyes opened. The air was thick and humid. The pores of my skin broke out into beads of sweat. Swimming might be a possibility. But then, I noticed I was the only one in the trailer. There was a chorus of voices coming from outside the door of the camper. Something was not right.

I dressed in my pants and opened the door. Big drops of water from the tented flap hit my head. In unison the teachers, along with my father, mother, brother, and sister, were staring up the hill at a small canvas tent. Camping gear spread around as if thrown in a fit of anger. The iron rods that had just yesterday held the tent upright were twisted, leaning at unusual angles as if the tent had been mauled by a bear.

The family's tent had been struck by lightning and the teachers told my dad that the father of the family was paralyzed from the waist down.

The thought of not being able to move one's legs horrified me. I slid my hands in my pockets and pinched the skin of my own legs. My sockless feet could feel the ground's coolness as I stepped in place.

The teachers must have seen our panic descend. Dead silence, not even the sound of a breath, it was as if my whole family was paralyzed.

"He probably won't be paralyzed for long," said the tallest teacher as he turned and spoke to us.

"Huh?" I squeaked.

"The guy will have more problems than paralysis. That most likely will go away." He went on to explain that he had taken many courses in wilderness medicine and had learned that if struck by lightning something called the autonomic nervous system would become overloaded, but with time, would eventually recalibrate. Deep burns, possibly damaged internal organs were to be bigger problems. He added, "If we were ever caught in an open field when a thunderstorm hit it was best to be still, crouch down and make yourself as small as possible. It takes only .5 of a second for lighting to strike." My fear leaked away: counting and crouching felt like common sense.

The teachers turned and headed back to their campsite. They were in a hurry, lots of miles to travel. My mother began flitting between the tent trailer and the picnic table wiping away puddles and setting out breakfast foods. She called for my sister and I to set the table. My dad and brother headed towards the back of the tent trailer looking to see if there had been any damage. Not likely my father explained, we had rubber tires. I yelled after them, would we be able to go swimming today, was today the day?

A far-reaching aha moment occurred several years later, as if the lightning strike had settled itself into my subconscious, a memory that was smoldering with energy, wonder, and power.

I was in Edmonton, Alberta, Canada. It was wintertime. My track club had traveled there by train—a long sleepless night across the frozen prairies to a newly built fieldhouse, a cavernous building that held a 200-meter tartan oval track. It was modern and a perfect place for the Canadian indoor championships. The previous fall we had collected used bottles and cashed them in to raise money to pay our expenses. I believe we stayed in the dorms at the university, not an expensive proposition, but one that our bottle drive and the collection of nickels and dimes could pay for.

I was 16 years old, 120 pounds, five feet, five inches tall, and I was tired—a heaviness from not getting my usual sleep. Sleeping on the train had been impossible. Even with my eyes closed I became aware of a litany of discomforts: my body barely fit inside the top bunk that swayed back and forth accompanied by a never-ending clickity-clack. My ears never stopped hearing metal on metal for twenty-three hours.

Our track uniform—navy blue shorts and white shirts with Galaxy written diagonally across the front, was made from a thick cloth that poked at my skin. I itched, but I was warm. The polished confidence of my competitors swarmed around me. The one who was in the lane next to mine had traveled from Vancouver. Probably by airplane. She had made national teams and had competed in far-off exotic countries, expenses paid for by the government and not by a month of Saturdays hauling bottles. How did I ever believe that I could beat them? My times from past races were slower and yet, here I was. Somehow, I had qualified for the 50-meter final. I was to run in lane two. The reigning national champion was to run in lane three.

Earlier, I had begun my warm-up jogging slowly around the inside of the oval track. I went through my routine—running laps, stretching, practicing my starts from the blocks, what I had done many, many times before. I felt stiff and clunky, as a thick muscular tension overtook my body, effortlessness swallowed by fear. Losing seemed likely, confirmed by the words of my coach. Just the day before, he had asked me when I was going to find the will to win.

I sagged deeper into tiredness and then, as I hit rock bottom, I ratcheted my body and unfolded my posture until I stood ramrod straight. It was not a matter of finding the will to win! Hadn't I always wanted to win?

I closed my eyes and imagined the race I was about to run. I would be the first out of my blocks accompanied by a crack and a sizzle. All at once, I felt an idea surging through my body, a possibility, a sense that I could strike like a flash of lightning. A wave of giddiness descended—the crack of a lightning strike overruled the words of my coach.

Many years later, I studied the biomechanics of world class male sprinters as they went from their starting blocks to the first steps of their race. Scientists had broken the skill into three discrete events: reaction time, both legs push, front leg push, all of this took .5 of a second, the speed of a lightning strike.

The starter called out our names. As I stood behind my starting blocks, I stared at the familiar tracksuits of the

Canadian national team. Red and white like the Canadian flag with "Canada" in silk red letters across the front of the jacket. I would give anything to wear that uniform. The competitors took off the tracksuits to reveal their local track club uniforms, everyone wearing a thin silky polyester uniform that flowed with their every move.

Everyone, including me, had long hair tied back in a ponytail. As we practiced our starts for one last time, their ponytails flopped every which way along with a knowing kind of laughter—wise and used to winning, to being successful. They had traveled to places that I had only read about in books. From head to toe, they knew things I didn't know. But these were thoughts that I swatted away as I envisioned the speed of the lightning strike.

With a big breath I narrowed my gaze and set my blocks. Using my feet as a yardstick, a strategy taught to me by Mr. Lucas, I measured the distance from the starting line and positioned the edge of the block alongside the tip of my toe. A foot and a half for the right block, three feet for the left. I practiced one or two starts: pushing on the blocks, accelerating, body rising, arms pumping, and letting my tongue slip into the roof of my mouth. No grimacing or head wagging, no fear, just my body striking with lightning speed at the crack of the starting pistol.

"On your marks."

I bend down and fold inwards, tap the ground with the toes of my shoes and place them onto the blocks along with the rest of my forefoot, my familiar toe-walking now re-configured. My fingers form a tripod a hair's breadth behind the starting line. Electric charges run through my body.

"Get set."

My body weight rocks forward on to my tripod eager to spend its pent-up energy.

Bang.

An eruption of limbs, low, outward bound and the strike of my first footfall, powering my body forward. Before the next blink of an eye my body soars and slices through the air. My feet felt as if they never touched the ground.

Out of the corner of my eye, a black ponytail. Stride, stretch, lean, a flailing of arms and legs that felt nothing like what I had seen on television, had never practiced, an instant that I now know I had been unprepared for.

Just before the all-important lean, not only the ponytail but also a flash of a green, the color of my competitor's jersey.

Later, my coach told me that my start had beaten everyone. My lean was the moment when I had lost the race. But I knew that I had found how to perform a fast start, and it had nothing to do with the will to win. I wondered if he knew anything about the art of the lean.

I had run one of the fastest times in Canada, almost half a second faster than my personal best. I had been close, only a blink of an eye separated me from winning and becoming a Canadian champion.

It was the lean, I had to get better at the lean. I could strike with the speed of lighting, sprint with the joy of effortlessness, and now I just needed to find the right combination of leaning and timing, to gain the hundredths of a second that would lead to victory. To be prepared and responsible, to erase the fear of losing—I had unleashed the mystery of my athletic self. Trusting my body was how I was going to achieve my Olympic dream.

CHAPTER TEN

Civil Unrest and Protests: Mexico Games 1968

"O sport you are Justice! The perfect fairness
which men seek in vain in their social institutions
rises around you of its own accord…"
Pierre de Coubertin

The story of just how important sport was to a city and to Canadians began with their national sport, hockey. In 1951, four years before I was born, the Canadian men's hockey team lost to the Americans at the 1956 Winter Games in Cortina d'Ampezzo, Italy. The media headlines were distraught. There had been literal and metaphorical weeping. Outrage targeted the performance of the players, deemed to be at fault for a collective national shame over losing.

Since the end of WWII, the idea that sport mattered more than we could know, was taking hold. Politicians were considering the many benefits to the nation of hosting global sporting events, which often came with the promise of building new sporting facilities. Winnipeg had a core of sports enthusiasts, physical educators, and university professors that volunteered to make a bid to host the Pan Am Games in 1967.

They succeeded.

By all accounts, discontent was also growing amongst amateur athletes who wanted financial support from the federal government. Athletes whose families could not afford to support them as they trained struggled to be competitive. To be-the-best-that-they-could be, they needed time, space, and money. Winning for your country was worth the price for taxpayers.

The year after the 1968 Mexico Games, the task force on Sport for Canadians published a report, a policy statement, which recommended among other dictums, an end to the strictest definition of amateurism, a boon for athletes who had limited financial means. Other recommendations proposed sport governing bodies that would manage national and international competitions, as well as membership associations that would support the development of coaches and elite athletes and that would bring together professionals with expertise in sports medicine. Federal dollars were to provide all the funding. Politicians acted quickly, establishing Sport Canada as a department of the National Health and Welfare in 1971. By then, the city of Montreal had been chosen by the IOC to host the 1976 summer Games.

In the end, many Canadians and politicians thought these ideas and recommendations would result in gold medal performances at the Olympic Games, a boon to national unity and the well-being of a Canadian national identity. Everyone assumed that the demonstration of excellence in sport would also inspire Canadians to participate in fitness and sport at the recreational level. A centralized, governmental control that would benefit all Canadians.

Eventually, these changes would result in some surprises for me. Over the next four years, as the policies took shape, the Canadian Track and Field Association, sent me telegrams notifying me that I was a 'C' student athlete, the lowest ranking. In recognition of my sprinting potential, no doubt a result of my now-famous-in-my-mind Edmonton race, I was awarded a one-time grant to be used toward training costs. With that money and the advice of my father, I bought a car that allowed me to travel from the arena to school and to home, and sometimes the training facilities at the University, legacy facilities built for the 1967 Pan Am Games. No more long bus rides. I now had time to train for the Montreal Games, complete my school homework and get a good night's sleep. The government had invested in my Olympic dream.

The backdrop to these political changes in Canada was the mysterious events of the 1968 Mexico Games. During this time, the idea that sport mattered took the dueling narratives of the meaning of Olympism to an unimaginable place. Violence shaped the backdrop of our lives, brought to us by news broadcasts filled with reports of the civil rights protests in the US. A nightly barrage of images spilling out from TV screens: marching protesters brought under control by baton-wheeling policemen, bloodied heads, shouting, and spitting, crying and siren calls. Absolute chaos. What we did not see was the growing student protests in Mexico, protests aimed at government corruption associated with the planning for the Games. Corruption had robbed the students of their education along with future opportunities to be-the-best-they-could-be.

Far from the global camera's reach, sports reporter John Rodda, who worked for the *The Guardian*, had come to Mexico early. On October 2, he went to Tlatelolco plaza to report on the student protests that had been gaining momentum. The police occupied the Polytechnic as soldiers rimmed nearby rooftops. He made his way toward an apartment building where student protesters spoke from a balcony. After showing his press credentials, he found a spot to observe the events of the day. He listened for about forty-five minutes as the square began to swell with protesters. And then, military helicopters appeared. Soon after, he was pushed face down on a stony floor ducking a hail of bullets.

For several hours the military controlled the building where he had hunkered down. After his release, he filed the story with his newspaper–a first-hand account that he subsequently followed up with a commentary on whether the Games should continue. Chaos prevailed; the government blamed the students for conspiring to disrupt the Games, which they disputed. They wanted to reform their repressive government; they wanted more opportunities to learn. Over 500 were people murdered, probably many more tortured and jailed in the aftermath. Avery Brundage, the then president of the International Olympic Committee, ignored what had happened, declaring that on the night of the massacre, he had been at the ballet. He saw no reason for the Games to be cancelled. Mexican Olympic officials declared a news blackout; the blood and rubble of the massacre removed. Spectators and national teams arrived. The drama of the upcoming competitions overruling the horrific events of the massacre.

Only forty years later, would I learn of what happened that day. Most athletes and spectators remained ignorant of the unspeakable, or feared severe consequences if they spoke about what they knew to be true. Later, Bruno Balke would tell the story of Roger Jackson, one of his graduate students from Canada, who was competing in Mexico in the rowing competitions despite becoming sick after eating out at a local restaurant. Mexico was also to be Harry Jerome's last international competition in the 100-meters. Did they see the bloodied square? Hear the horror stories? Or did they focus on their competitions? Did the veil of silence make the massacre invisible to them?

October 12th, a warm fall Saturday afternoon. Raking the leaves became an afterthought as we prepared to watch a live broadcast of the Games. TV tables dotted the living room, brown trays that clipped onto golden fold-away legs. They wobbled if you cut your food too vigorously. My mother, who was working full time at a retail store, had discovered frozen TV dinners, and reasoned a way to her own version. As the hour approached for both dinner and the Games, we would reheat the tin-foiled plates and carry them to our assigned TV table and watch the sport spectacles unfold.

Drama as it happened drew us like bees to honey, even though our TV screen by this time had a dusky yellowish hue, which I reasoned was due to Mexico's hot weather and high altitude. By now satellite broadcasting was in its infancy allowing North American viewers to watch the games live and in color. Mexico was the most televised and filmed Games to date.

My parents had opinions about the startling iconic posters. It made them uncomfortable as if the black and white patterned art of the indigenous Huichol people vibrated before their eyes. I wondered if athletes attended the festivals of art that lined the roadways from the Olympic village to the Aztec stadiums. You could not miss the juxtaposition of color and shape, arranged symmetrically or with a puzzling randomness. As the TV camera swept between posters and the festival, it felt disorientating, just like the fun houses I explored when the circus came to Winnipeg.

I sat at my TV table and watched the long jumpers take flight. Drama first occurred at lift off from the board. Stepping over the edge of the board, even just the width of a hair, would disqualify that jump. With each competitor I studied their run, high knees, and a bounding gallop that looked nothing like an effortless sprint. Next the launch. Arms and legs thrown up and forward, reaching for a mark. Here I made a quick sideways glance at the official, a man dressed in a wrinkled suit and a fedora holding the ominous red flag. Would he raise the red flag of disqualification? And then back to the athlete, who by now hit the sand, momentum all but stopped. Sometimes they fell sideways, and, if something had gone wrong, backwards.

The officials measured from the launching board to the indentations in the sand. Falling backwards could cut off feet, not inches, from their jump. I'm sure I held my breath, and then the announcer exclaimed the results, the pitch of his voice determined by just how close a jumper came to winning a medal.

Bob Beamon, the American long jumper, who at one time had lost his athletic scholarship because of his protesting the assassination of Martin Luther King, stood at the beginning of the runway, concentration etched into his face. He had a tall, well-proportioned, lean body. His loose fitting dark colored shirt hung across his upper body with USA in big red letters, a sagging soft cloth number, 254, was pinned to his shirt. He wore white baggy shorts that looked as if they had just come out of the washing machine. The run, the launch, and then his body folding in half, soaring for long seconds, longer than anyone before him. No red flag, and then the landing, falling forward with only a slight lean to the right.

Silence invaded the living room followed by the excited voice of the broadcaster. The new electronic recording tools employed at the Games for the first time were unable to measure the jump. We waited twenty minutes for the officials to locate a tape measure. Finally, an official announcement: the jump measured 8.90 meters, 55 centimeters farther than the world record. Later, we would learn that physicists reasoned that the high altitude of Mexico made it easier to jump so far. It seemed like an Aesop Fable, a fairy tale about the impossible coming true. The world record would never have happened if not for Beamon's extraordinary talent, but it would be a record with an asterisk linked to three words–'*achieved at altitude.*'

Three athletes that had medaled in the men's 100 meters at the Mexico Games, combined their dramatic performances with a civil rights protest. Tommie Smith and John Carolos, joined by Australian sprinter Peter Norman, stood barefooted with raised fists on the podium as the American National Anthem was played. They wore black gloves, a symbol of support for the Black Panther movement in America. The disdain over their protest was as energetic as Beamon's remarkable feat.

Olympic officials worked to crush the careers of the three men. The world of sport was adamant. The Games transcended politics and civil unrest. But no matter how indignant the IOC became, history would tell another story, the Games have always been political, the brotherhood of man a secondary concern.

The untold stories of corruption, violence and bullying eventually would find the global stage. In retrospect they signaled the power of politics over sport shamelessly mingling with spell-binding dramatic athleticism. And in time, the voices of athletes would soon engage with the civil unrest as physical educators or political actors.

After 1968, Harry Jerome began his career as a teacher, a role model for young athletes and those that dream of becoming an Olympian. He also worked for Sport Canada developing a nation-wide tour of demonstration sports, an ambassador for the sport-for-all version of Olympism.

By 1976, after completing his graduate program with Bruno Balke, Roger Jackson would become Director of Sport Canada. From 1978 to 1988 he was Dean of the Faculty of Kinesiology at the University of Calgary. And then from 1982 through 1990 the President for the Canadian Olympic Committee. He became the ambassador for excellence in sport, a priority. Sport-for-all was of secondary importance.

Bruce Kidd, a friend of both Jerome and Jackson, had started his career at the University of Toronto, and soon became embroiled with federal and provincial political forces that had won their bid to host the Games of 1976 in Montreal. It would be an opportunity for him to join the playing fields of sport with the world of art, similar to the vision of Coubertin. He worked to include public events at the Games that would involve recreational athletes; and canvassed Olympic hopefuls as to their financial status as amateurs; they were starving, depending on families for financial support, some had resorted to stealing food. He then worked with other former athletes in advocating for Canada's Olympic hopefuls, eventually being involved in protests that threatened a boycott of the '76 Games by athletes. His activism resulted in former Canadian Olympians being given administrative positions in institutions that governed the lives of amateur athletes.

Athletes' voices had found their way into the politics of sport: Kidd, Jackson, and Jerome, each in their own way, taking up either the win-at-all-costs or the-best-that-one-can-be narratives. It was a time where the dueling narratives seemed destined to find a common ground, but everyone would soon realize that they had underestimated the grip that winning-at-all-costs had on the future of sports in Canada.

CHAPTER ELEVEN

Win-at-All-Costs: The Science of Oxygen Delivery

"In the field and in the laboratory, Bruno Balke
proved that the human body in prime condition could
achieve amazing things, exerting himself to levels
greater than even the experts would have predicted."
Author Maura Phillips Mackowski

The mark of an asterisk was followed by the words *'achieved at altitude,'* highlighting the drama of world or Olympic record performances at the Mexico Games. The asterisk, meaning *little star*, rooted in the language of ancient Greece, was the preferred shorthand for the science of the win-at-all-costs untold story. Beside the asterisk were numbers quantifying the time, distance, or height achieved by a human being, an amazing story. Or as Coubertin predicted, the sport record was *'inescapably the summit of the sport edifice.'*

The common beliefs that surrounded the vagaries of general fitness training, were coming under scrutiny at the University of Wisconsin in Madison. By early 1964, Balke had gained a reputation as an expert in the developing field of exercise science, and had become the president-elect of the newly forming American College of Sports Medicine. He had established a program in bio-dynamics, a holistic rigorous examination of aerobic metabolism that mirrored his single-mindedness. He had survived whatever fate sent his way: hunger and starvation, bombings from Allied forces in Berlin and Paris, enemy fire while traveling to and from the front line, long periods of separation from his wife and children, infectious hepatitis, and a lightning strike while on a mountaineering expedition to the Himalayas; he not only survived, but he also thrived.

His daughter wrote a testimonial for his biography: "I had no idea my father was special, though he did seem to be a bit superhuman at times. He could hold so still that birds would come to eat out of his hand. He believed angels were watching over him, one of which was his deceased sister, Emmie, who advised him to pray more."

I read his words with the same wonder as his daughter. Fate had dealt him many blows and yet he continued to search for answers exposing himself and research subjects to environmental extremes that led to physical harm. Today's world of science would never allow this no-pain-no-gain ideal of athletics to be a guiding principle for research.

The imprecise ideas of general fitness had been codified. Balke had written a numerical story about the delivery of oxygen to working muscles that gave credence to the grueling workouts measured by stopwatches and fueled by the no-pain-no-gain mantra. It would become the exhaustive details that would lead to gold medal performances.

Officials involved in the planning for the Mexico Games chalked up many firsts: the first Games to be held in Latin America, the first to be held on an all-weather track, the first to use electronic timing equipment, and the first to provide live color broadcasts of the games to both European and North American audiences. It was also the first to be held at high altitude which created an opportunity for Balke's research to find a global stage.

Jack Daniels was a graduate student in Balke's lab. He was known as a tough competitor, a veteran soldier of the Korean War, whose fitness training, the proverbial boot camp experience, had taken on a mythic status. He competed in the modern pentathlon team event in two Olympics: Melbourne in 1956 and Rome in 1960, winning silver and bronze medals.

Before joining Balke's lab, Daniels had studied with basic scientists in Stockholm, doing research on isolated preparations, deconstructing the role of the heart from the working muscle during exertion. Upon his return from Sweden, he enrolled in prerequisite courses in physical education and physiology which would eventually lead to a PhD in the program headed by Balke. Balke's more whole-body vision and Daniels' isolated muscle research experience fostered a unique collaboration.

Daniels' success at the Olympics had also gained him entry to a circle of friends that included American middle- and long-distance runners vying for Olympic gold in Mexico. He had recruited them and trained them at high altitude several years before the Mexico Games. He knew the number story needed for success in Mexico.

In 1965, Balke, Daniels, and co-author Fran Nagle, published a paper of their findings, a recipe for adaptation to altitude that would benefit middle- and long-distance runners, including the American favored to win the 1500-meter race in Mexico, Jim Ryun. The results of their research showed that the lower pressure of oxygen at high altitudes resulted in a diminished oxygen content of the blood. With exertion, oxygen debt would be quickly incurred by the athletes, resulting in a devastating loss of energy. Training at altitude for prescribed blocks of time, described by Balke's research, allowed the body to adapt to the lower oxygen content of the blood. It was a complicated story with a fairy-tale ending: bodies could acclimate to extreme environments.

U.S. officials feared that high altitude training for weeks at a time was akin to being paid to train, putting an athlete's amateur status at risk. The American Olympic Committee, even after hearing presentations by Balke on the impact of high altitude on performance, disallowed Ryun, and other Olympic hopefuls, from attending training camps at high altitude. The expectations for Ryun to win a gold medal in Mexico were high. The year before, he had set the world record for the 1500 meters. His signature finishing kick thrilled Americans, the best example of a come-from-behind victory.

As the track and field events began in Mexico, it became clear that performances were impacted by the high altitude. Even in those sports that required short bursts of energy, world records fell by the wayside aided by the thin rarefied air that offered less resistance to sprinting and long jumping. Long- and middle-distance runners, however, were hampered by the low oxygen content of the air. They literally fell by the wayside as officials rushed bottles of oxygen to their sides.

Ryun tells the story that before the final in the 1500-meter race, he felt terrible, exhausted from the qualifying rounds. To add to his difficulties, he was recovering from an ankle injury as well as mononucleosis.

The race began with South African runner Ben Jipco setting a blistering pace. The plan, developed by Jipco and Keno, was to lure Ryun into keeping close to the pace that would then throw him into oxygen debt, limiting the power of his signature race-ending kick. It worked. In spite of running a personal best, Ryun came in second and Kip Keno won with a new world record. Keno had spent his life living in the higher altitudes of the Nandi Hills in Western Kenya.

In 1966, another athlete had joined Balke's cadre of graduate students. Kidd's colleague, Roger Jackson, a rower, had found, in Madison, the perfect place to train: in the winter at an indoor rowing pool and in the summer on Lake Mendota.

He competed in Tokyo, Japan, in 1964, winning a gold medal, and in 1966 joined Balke's bio-dynamics PhD program. In 1968 he had set his sights on Mexico. Both Balke and Jackson trained together every morning from the middle of May until the end of the summer, as well as spending time altitude training at Lake Dillon, Colorado. Balke attended a sports medicine conference in Mexico at the time Roger competed, and watched as Jackson's gold medal quest was foiled by a bout with dysentery. It was as if Jackson's performance could be marked with an asterisk explaining how fate, despite his optimistic attitude, had foiled his dream.

After Jackson's athletic career had ended, he became involved with Sport Canada and various Canadian Olympic Committees, and led the movement that focused on aiding student athletes so that they could achieve excellence in sport. He was seen as an Olympic hero who knew what it took to win gold medals, and he dedicated himself to creating conditions so that Canadian athletes could compete at the international level and win medals. Excellence meant paying attention to things you had control over, like where and how you trained and what you ate. Being the-best-you-could-be seemingly linked arms with excellence, with the caveat that controlling what you could was imperative.

Balke and colleagues had set the physiological parameters that athletes needed to attain for elite performance. Jackson would spend the rest of his career providing Canadian athletes with the environment and facilities needed to reach the highest goals. Elite performance would become attached to the bounties of an expanding sports-media complex, rather than the aesthetic ethic rooted in creativity and the joy of movement that motivated athletes to push themselves to the limits of their abilities.

Fate continued to haunt Jackson's career. Presumably, he learned of the Tlatelolco massacre, which may have given him pause to remember the Munich massacre and how close he was to the hostage taking that led to the death of eleven of his fellow athletes. Then, as an Olympic official in 1988, he was the leader of the Canadian delegation that had to manage the aftermath of the drug doping scandal of Ben Johnson, which was not just Canada's scandal. Six of eight runners in that 100-meter final, at some time in their careers, would test positive for banned substances. The science of drug testing, by 1988, had hit its stride.

In 1968, my family cheered for our hero Harry Jerome and watched as he placed seventh in the 100-meter final. We decided that it had something to do with the high altitude, but later his coach would say that he thought Jerome had been ill-prepared to run. American Jim Hines was the gold medalist and had broken the ten-second mark, a world record. The announcers began to call him the *'fastest man alive.'* But it was noted that all the world record performances of Mexico were to be recorded with an asterisk linked forever to the words: *'achieved at high altitude.'*

I voiced my opinion to my father, even though I had not the inkling of an idea what the impact of high altitude could mean—Hines had run his personal best, a world's best, it was not fair—my newly-found, whiny mantra. He probably said something like, *'don't get carried away,'* parent-speak for life-is-not-fair. I probably shrugged his words to the back of my mind.

CHAPTER TWELVE

Being the-Best-You-Can-Be: The Science of Oxygen Delivery

> "A measurement of perceived exertion refers to an individual's inner state and the intensity that this state has in the individual's frame of reference. Thus, it does not primarily depend on [the intensity of exercise] but more on the 'absolute' inner feeling."
>
> *Gunnar Borg*

Kipchoge Keino, a man who had grown up on the high plains of Kenya herding goats, who ran the four miles to and from school in bare feet, who had no specialized coaching, beat Jim Ryun by 20 meters, the largest margin in the history of the race. His childhood sense of athleticism had won the day.

It must have been galling for Balke and Daniels to watch Jim Ryun's 1500-meter race. Balke had spent his career parsing the details between the role of the heart muscle and the skeletal muscle. Fitness in number-speak was defined as the volume of oxygen transported by each heartbeat and the efficiency of how it was utilized by muscle. It became the holy grail of athleticism, a number labeled as VO_2 max, that summed up the cardiovascular system's abilities and that became equated with the pace and speed to achieve the elite performance. Their thinking and Ryun's abilities should have combined to bring home the coveted gold medal that Americans expected.

In retrospect however, Ryun did run a personal best despite his lack of high-altitude training—an astonishing accomplishment that their numbers could not account for. Ryun had waged a heroic battle to fight the pain of oxygen debt.

Ryun's race personified the thrill of victory and the agony of defeat, Jim McKay's famous tagline. The TV broadcast of the race focused on his every step. Reporting on his grueling workouts, his lean body, his reputation to win with an amazingly powerful finishing kick, how the year before he had set a new world record for the 1500-meters at sea level. Oxygen debt was discussed with wild anxiety. Probably the first time I had heard these words as I watched the Games. Oxygen debt was invisible, a bad guy that threatened Olympic heroes.

To determine an athletes' VO_2 max, Balke and his graduate student Jack Daniels used titrated protocols on treadmills. They were able to control the speed and elevation of the treadmill and in a stepwise manner, increase the intensity of the exercise while measuring the amount of oxygen consumed. The athletes would be pushed to their absolute limit of exertion, *'not able to take another step'* was the end point of the protocol.

But something was not adding up: athletes were telling Daniels that they noticed running on the treadmill was harder than running at the same pace on the track. Daniels had experienced the same thing. Three miles on the track adhering to pace felt harder than running the same distance on a golf course when given free rein to manage the effort, speeding up and slowing down at will. The same distance covered in the same time, but it somehow felt easier.

The perception of exertion—how hard it felt to run— did not match what the equations that Balke and Daniels had labored over would predict. An equation that considered the perception of exertion, a holistic equation, was something they had not imagined.

Gunnar Borg, a 400-meter sprinter from Sweden who once had an Olympic dream, had published and lectured widely on the rating of perceived exertion scales based on his research with subjects performing all levels of activity. He also served as a member of the research council for sports in Sweden, and in the 1960s had turned his science towards the elite athlete. Unbeknownst to him, he would find that his scales measuring perception of exercise would become relevant to both elite athletic performance and being the-best-you-could-be. A science story that would become the link between the dueling narratives.

The story of oxygen debt began in the days of Coubertin. A.V. Hill, considered the father of exercise science, delivered his Nobel speech with a mixture of science and a hint of poetry. He explained, "One knows that after violent exercise one breathes heavily for some time: the more violent the exercise, the longer one's respiration is labored."

Two years later, he wrote in a scientific paper, "...if the exercise be so severe that its oxygen requirement [of muscle] cannot be met ...by the respiratory circulatory system...the body goes into debt for oxygen...enormous oxygen debts are sometimes found in man, sometimes up to 19 liters, and imply an accumulation of lactic acid in muscles... and other organs and... [needing] a long process of recovery."

Borg had observed that when subjects were asked how hard they were working, they evaluated the effort by the fatigue of their muscles and their labored breathing.

Borg's work involved a series of experiments that unearthed how these perceptions of exertions, when rated numerically by subjects, corresponded to the numerical description of heart rate. Borg knew that when the subjects rated the exercise '17' when using a scale that ranged from 1-21, it roughly corresponded to a heart rate of 170, which was considered sub-maximal exercise for a healthy person. So, he anchored the number 17 with the words *very hard* as a descriptor of the exercise intensity. The lowest number of the scale '6,' corresponded to a resting heart rate of 60. He then set word anchors to every uneven number from 6-17. *Very light* was '9,' whereas as '13,' associated with a heart rate of 130, was labeled *somewhat hard.* '19,'—*extremely hard* (heart rate 190), and '20,'—maximal exertion.

The results of Borg's experiments suggested that the athlete's sense of exertion was a perception of the workings of his body that was relative to workload, but that also varied depending on the fitness level of the person. The same workload could be perceived very differently depending on environmental factors, and the athleticism of the subject. But much to the astonishment of exercise scientists, when subjects were given the freedom to vary their pace of exercise using Borg's RPE scale rather than an intensity governed by a set protocol, they varied their work rate. It was as if they were getting ready for the final push at the end of a race, a strategy to find the best number to describe their maximum oxygen-carrying capacity, a strategy used by Kidd and Ryun to conserve their energy for their signature finishing kick. It was the secret to winning, at least some of the time, and to achieving the highest VO_2 max.

Testing protocols devised by Balke dictated the speed, time, and workload of exercise, thus imposing a numerical ideal of athleticism. But when research subjects were allowed to select their own pace and intensity, an unconscious link to athleticism was given free reign. Surprisingly, the measured VO_2 max was higher than found under Balke's standardized protocols. This is a conclusion that to this day is considered controversial and will undoubtedly need more research. The never-ending story of science had begun to bridge the gap between the dueling narratives.

The holy grail of fitness testing, the VO_2 max, remains the target. How it is measured and tested now must consider the human subjective sense of exercise. In other words, the to-be-the-best-that-you-can-be mindset was starting to appear as a powerful factor in the win-at-all-costs, no-pain-no-gain, training regimes. The mindset for competition to be governed by strain and fatigue, a sense of breathlessness and increasing heart beats, a body signaling its power to push itself to its limit.

There is no record that Balke met Borg. It is possible by their connections to the world of exercise science, and their past involvement in the Games, that they may have sat somewhere over a beer and casually talked about their work. A happenstance that led them to think deeper and question their science. Or maybe they studied each other's published papers, sitting in their respective academic libraries, embedded in comfy chairs, taking time to read the emerging story of exercise science. Collectively, their work and their passions created a river of possibilities. Athletes and patients with heart disease, or any disease where fatigue was an obstacle to healing, would benefit. Perception of exertion and effortlessness mattered.

In 1966, Balke would begin to explore his science and question the dogma of chair therapy after a heart attack. He began working with heart patients soon after he presented his research to cardiologists. They sent him their patients with damaged hearts, and he methodically improved their functional capacity, now a group of words attached to the limitations of oxygen delivery caused by a weakened heart. This is nowhere close to maximum VO_2, in most cases, but an idea that was guided by the perception of exercise.

Daniels went on to build a life coaching athletes at all levels, recreational, collegiate, and the elite, succeeding in developing world class female distance runners. He was known for his expertise at motivating athletes by his philosophy of training. He angled away from the no-pain-no-gain mantra of the Nurmi, Zápotek, Landy, and Kidd crowd towards being-the-best-you-can be. His mantra: do the minimum amount of work for the maximum payoff.

In hindsight, it probably was no surprise to Borg, Balke, or Daniels. Perceptions married to physiology was a story that they had experienced as Olympic hopefuls. It was becoming the backdrop to everyone's stories.

Spectators, estimated in the millions, understood it as a dramatic story that they could watch live on television, and for the first time at the Mexico Games in color. The numbers were mind-boggling: five thousand athletes from 112 countries descended on Mexico City. It was the first-time athletes would be tested for drug doping. American Wyomia Tyus won a career second gold medal in the 100-meters, and a large number of records were set in sports that required short bursts of intense effort: jumping, throwing, weightlifting, and sprinting. No one expressed certainty what the high altitude would do to athletes, so any, and all, distance races were tinged with the drama of bottles of oxygen lying beside gasping, prostrate, athletes.

As we watched the 1968 Games, neither my father nor I knew anything of this science story. It would weave its way through time, right up to the moment I was to run the race that determined if I had a chance to be selected for the Montreal Games. It was the way of my world; my body would learn it first as it wrote the story of my intuitive athleticism. It would be my common sense and good sense until it no longer made any sense.

I ignored the talk of oxygen debt and downplayed its invisibility to slay an Olympic hero. Instead, I followed the joy-filled perch of my toe-walking, privileging my perceptions of the world that made me feel special. As I watched the Mexico Games unfold, I decided that oxygen debt was a mysterious foe, it was a sense that now invaded my dreams where I feared losing, pummeling the hallway wall with more vigor, probably waking my parents. Oxygen debt was a scientific truth that would complicate my Olympic Dream.

CHAPTER THIRTEEN

Competing Against International Athletes

"We are such stuff as dreams are made of…"
William Shakespeare

Late one Sunday morning in the Spring of 1972, I was reading in bed. The spring floodwaters had finally receded, and the competitive summer season loomed. Fresh air mixed with the smell of lilacs wafted through my bedroom window, a ritual of spring my mother enforced religiously. The phone, attached to the wall in the hallway, rang out. I scrambled out of bed and ran to answer it. Going to church was on the agenda. Who in heaven's name would be calling my family on a Sunday morning?

"Hello, my name is June. I'm the secretary for the Canadian National Track and Field Association."

"Umm…" June was a season and not a name. Phone pranks—the latest fad amongst the boys in my class.

"You've been selected to run the 4x100 meter relay on the Canadian women's sprint team traveling this July. Two weeks competing at track and field meets in Germany and the Netherlands."

I gulped back a breath of air. The voice—a no fooling around kind—was not a teenage boy. "Details will follow by telegram." The phone line went dead.

Later, my coach would tell me that the 50-meter second place finish at the national indoor championship had gotten me noticed. Probably not for Munich, but Montreal…maybe.

Traveling by airplane to Europe. My dream comes true.

My mother leapt into action soon after the telegram arrived, and dates and places confirmed. We went shopping to buy a '*traveling suit,*'—a chocolate brown jacket and pants matched with a beige short-sleeved sweater. Journalists came to a twilight track meet at the Pan Am stadium and took my picture wearing a goofy sun hat. They wrote about my possibilities for the Montreal Games and my excitement to travel to Europe. My father started a scrapbook and pasted that article to one of its pages. And workouts got easier as my coach spent more time talking about the fanfare of international competition than requiring me to run the dreaded time trials.

The night before I left to join the team, my aunt and my hockey-playing uncle arrived, just in time for dinner. They gave me a present, a small silver pin in the shape of a maple leaf. In 1965 a red maple leaf on a white background became Canada's new national flag replacing the old colonial version. There had been many dinnertime conversations about Canada's independence from England. I thought the maple leaf was a good choice. I loved how its leaves turned golden red in the fall. As I fingered the pin, the details of the silvered maple leaf merged with the rustle of our new flag. I imagined I could hear the crowds singing the national anthem. Another version of my Olympic dream emerged.

In Toronto, I met up with the team and the head coach who was from a well-known track and field club in British Columbia. He was older, and most of the time he looked exhausted. He informed me that I would also be running the 100-meter sprint in addition to the relay. The best woman sprinter in Canada, who was also on the team, was recovering from shin splints. I would be running as her replacement. I don't remember that this bit of news scared me, probably because as he spoke with me, I also received my team uniform: soft cotton, bright red colors, a track suit that felt like a soft blanket. As I tried on my uniform and looked at myself in the mirror, I felt like I belonged, that I was good enough to be a part of the team.

On one of our first nights in Germany, I woke to the sound of voices coming from the hallway. Jet-lagged, after traveling overseas, my eyes took in the darkness while my body was eager to rise and shine. I got out of bed and took several minutes to open the door, clunk, and then clank, unlock, lock, over and over, until I figured out to turn the doorknob only as far as the sound of the clunk, and then push. I burst into the hallway just as laughter smothered itself behind straight-line grins. I slithered to the ground beside another sprinter who had already begun to inch sideways enlarging the space between us. Something was wrong, and it appeared to be me.

Conversations resumed: breaking curfew, smoking cigars, drinking pure vodka, and then the curious fact that they no longer menstruated, as if all women athletes should know this, and that their mothers were too dumb to see that they were not pregnant. I knew that I still had regular periods. None of it made sense. I concentrated on forming a wordless all-knowing expression. I studied my teammates wondering if they cared what Jim McKay would say about them on the *Wide World of Sports.*

More than ten thousand people came to watch our competitions held in the middle of the day at a large athletic stadium on the outskirts of Essen, Germany. The team rode from the dorm-style accommodations to the stadium in twenty taxis, small two-door sedans that could only hold two or three people. The javelin, too long to fit inside the cab, hung outside the car secured by the thrower's muscular arms. The narrow road wound through a thick forest, nighttime in the middle of the afternoon. Like clockwork, each taxi's headlights turned on. I could see the cars ahead of me weave their way through the forest, light to dark, a funeral procession cloaked in grief and not a team of gravity-defying competitors.

Spectators had overtaken the stadium. A rambunctious crowd formed near the start of the 100-meters. Spectators reached over the barriers waving their autograph books at me, calling out the name of the Canadian champion, in their broken English. She had medaled in the Pan Am games the year before in Cali, Columbia. I brushed past the spectators shaking my head no to their chanting, I was not who they thought I was. I scrambled to my lane and found myself bracketed by two women from East Germany, their bodies tall and thick, their expressions lifeless. Patches of dark wiry whiskers mottled their cheeks and chins. As they each took their lanes and began to set their blocks, the stink of sweat made it impossible to breathe deeply.

"Take your marks!" the starter called. I crouched down in front of the starting line as if I was watching *Wide World of Sports* and Jim McKay was making note of my race.

"Get Set!"

The gun sounded. A familiar push off from my blocks. Dead last. Thick muscular legs, feet pounding the ground, and guttural foreign cheers from the spectators. No heroic lean needed. I crossed the finish line upright, stunned and already feeling the flames of shame. I ran the race in my head many times and every time I came in dead last.

Shame descended again as I ran my leg of the 4x100-meter relay race. I almost dropped the baton in passing it to my teammate. The cheering for the winning home team felt like an oncoming thunderstorm.

The rest of the Canadian athletes did not fare much better. As we drove back to the dorms and then over dinner, the talking was intense as they told their version of just how the Canadian press would mock our poor performances. How journalists expected us to win to honor the nation, and yet had never reported on the lack of financial support to pay for coaches, physiotherapists, and state-of-the-art training facilities.

Later that night, as I lay in bed, my body wanted to sink into sleep while my mind ruminated over smelly sweat and mocking shame. No cool breeze of reason, no clarifying thoughts, nothing to take away confusion. What would my father, my mother, and Jim McKay say?

Later, to make matters worse, at one of the exhibition track meets, I jogged through the singing of the Canadian national anthem while immersed in my warm-up trying to conjure up the sense of absolute effortlessness. The coach said very little, but he looked as though he was going to disown me, leaving me to fare on my own in a foreign country. I felt like being forgotten in a foreign country was justified.

After I returned home, during one of our Sunday dinners, my father produced the scrapbook, the first few pages filled with newspaper articles and pictures of my European trip. The journalists hoped that I was on my way to becoming an elite Canadian sprinter. My father played with the blank pages, his flat hand smoothing them out as if preparing them for more 'documentation of my accomplishments. Their conversation swelled with an awkward rhythmic exuberance that I had never heard before. Common sense replaced by a full-throated barrage of good sense.

Their words soothed the pain of my humiliation, and when I answered their questions, I was careful to leave out the details of the parts of the trip that would alarm them. I ignored what I knew: I had been a token replacement for the champion with painful shin splints. If she wanted to run, I probably would never have been selected to the team.

I replayed my poor performances over and over again. Had it just been the weird food that had disturbed my competitiveness? My coach told me that my thinking about food was a sign that I was home sick. I craved peanut butter sandwiches, not a likely offering. But being homesick was also not likely. At one point we stayed at a dorm that was in the middle of a ragweed field, triggering my sleepless nights suffering from the ravages of allergies. I swallowed gallons of thick frothy snot. My appetite dwindled. Only food that tasted sweet passed my lips and not the bowls of cabbage soup and spicy stewed meat.

I never spoke of that nugget of fear that haunted my thoughts since I had come home. Was I just not good enough? Just a backup to the real athletes? It seemed obvious that I did not belong. I knew nothing compared to my teammates. My dreams frayed. I had traveled, a long-held part of my dream, to learn about the world, and what I had seen was nothing like what I had expected.

I shooed everyone away after dinner offering to make up for the times I missed the after-dinner cleanup. Alone in the semi-darkness, my hands immersed in soapy water, I handled the plates roughly. Hoisting myself onto the balls of my feet, I reasoned against the idea that I was not good enough.

Okay, the Jim McKay stories on *Wide World of Sports* were corny.

Okay, I was probably the country bumpkin that my teammates assumed.

Okay, not winning mattered because I had not done my best racing.

Did I not believe in a sound mind inside a sound body? That I was a responsible athlete having earned the trust of the government? That my truth would be fueled by the extraordinary: a gravity-defying pouf, a push-off followed by soaring and an expertly executed lean? I was a toe-walker, a natural born athlete, and I had the right stuff to make my dream come true.

My toe-walking was a story with a fairy-tale ending— even after the bad guys—the wicked step-mother, the big bad wolf, and the evil queens—had been discarded, done away with. Exactly how was I to overcome my fear and uncertainties, my personal collection of bad guys, when everything seemed so impossible?

I drained the dishwater, put the last of the dishes away in the cupboards, and turned towards the kitchen table where the scrapbook lay open. I fingered my way through the pages. Not winning, because I did not do my best, felt like I did not deserve a happy ending.

The words of the journalists, tight columns of black letters and patterned white space, the pride and beauty of the scrapbook began to overwhelm. Each page displayed my father's artistry—color, textures, and the detailed folds of the newspaper, carefully made to expose the headlines, the hopeful conclusions.

My parents and the sporting public also loved the happy ending, and now it was up to me to make it happen, to find the '*dream come true.*' Those oh so corny words of Jim McKay. Dreams were merely fairy tales, and the bad guys always held the fate-filled hand.

CHAPTER FOURTEEN

'Munich 1972 and Beyond'

"It was the Olympics, there are no borders."
Andrei Spitzer

September 5th, 1972, was likely among the first days of a new school year. I probably got up early and fretted as my brother, sister, and father circled around the one bathroom in the house. My mother would have been in the kitchen cooking oatmeal. Its smell fueled my impatience. It was imperative to eat the porridge when it was hot and gooey, swirling the melting brown sugar with a splash of milk. Timing was essential to cover up the horrid fishy taste of the cod liver oil pill mandated by my mother: sweet oatmeal, slimy pill, and then hot buttered toast. The mixture consumed in a precise order was a brilliant antidote to cod liver oil.

After breakfast, it would not have taken very long to gather my books and hurry out the door. I walked to school rather than ride my bike, avoiding the neighborhoods with dogs (I had been bitten once as a small girl). I entered the school and quickly walked downstairs to the hallway where the track team had their lockers, looking for teammates. Most of us were seniors in the university entrance program, excited to be back together and wondering if our track practice would be at Churchill Drive, a three-mile run that most of us hated. We traveled from class to class, discussing the possibilities, hoping that Churchill Drive was not in our future.

Across a continent and an ocean, the horror of the Munich Massacre unfolded. When exactly that day I would have heard about the eleven Israeli hostages I cannot recall. But I do remember that when I heard the news, the events unfolded in slow motion. Minute by minute a black hole overcame the merriment of a new school year. An ice-cold evilness washed over me with the relentless onslaught of evenly paced words reported by Jim McKay. I remember that I could barely avert my eyes even though I wanted to run away.

The Munich Massacre was a story that would work on me for the next forty-five years until what really happened that day was told by those who were there, unwitting witnesses to the loss of life. In 2016, *Munich 1972 and Beyond*, a documentary produced by Michael Cascio and Stephen Crisman was released. It told the story of the massacre and its aftermath, forty-four years' worth of facts dribbling out into the world.

It is a story narrated by Ankie Spitzer, the wife of murdered Andrei Spitzer, as she looked directly into the camera. Face to face with the audience the story she told echoed with her rage of injustice. She had spent her life seeking the truth, revealing the failure of Coubertin's ideals, and then elevating the voice of the murdered athletes as ambassadors for the true meaning of sport. Her face, angry yet stoic, her voice, harsh and empathetic as if she had one foot in the past and one in the present. As I watched the documentary, her presence held me in suspense. She knew the truth, and I trusted her to take me through the events of those horror filled days. Even though I knew the outcome, I sensed that she had more to teach me.

Munich 1972 and Beyond started with the facts: Israel was a young country that had only attended the Games six times. The athletes were children of holocaust survivors; they were Jewish. To be Olympians, they had to be good enough to have made an Olympic standard. A sprinting coach had been taken hostage; the athlete he coached had not.

The family room where I had convinced my father to let me attend public school, its orangeness everywhere, was where we watched most of the news coverage of the events of the massacre, was where our own set of facts hovered. My father's dictum on common sense and being responsible was sacred. We admired the athletes pursuing sport with their hard work and discipline. We understood when Jim McKay told stories of how people would delay weddings, and harvesting of crops, rearranging their lives to watch or attend the Games. We were joyful watching the Munich Games as it lived up to its billing as the Happy Games, the victory lap for German resilience to enter a modern world and leave their deadly past behind. We probably agreed that the absence of heavy security was proof that peace and brotherhood had arrived.

Later, untold stories crossed my path: the innovative stadium with its sweeping acrylic roof was built within eyeshot of Dachau; the manufacturer of WWII German bombs had been commissioned to make the Olympic torch; and construction of Olympic venues had unearthed undetonated bombs that were then exploded in the dark of night. I shuddered at what the German war generation thought as they heard the exploding bombs, possibly waking them from a deep sleep.

Munich 1972 and Beyond: Athletes gravitated to the spirit of a Happy Games, a place to gather in peace, '*a place with no borders,*' said Andrei Spitzer, an Israeli fencing coach who would later be murdered by the Palestinian group Black September.

His wife Ankie told the story of Andrei meeting with the fencing coach from Lebanon, then an enemy to Israel. Ankie was worried, but Andrei was reassuring, "This is the Olympics," he told her. He probably reminded her about the joy in participating in sport despite the hard work and discipline. The reward for his young athletes was the sense of exertion and the command and control of the saber. A common bond found between sportsmen. The Games transcended politics. Peace was on the horizon.

There are snippets of information that tell of how the athletes spent their days prior to the massacre. They had gone to visit Dachau. I imagine it must have felt like a cathartic moment—they had survived as a people and now they were building a brotherhood of peace through sport. I also learned that the night before the hostage-taking, they had seen *Fiddler on the Roof*, a musical, a love story that I had watched many times with my mother. It filled me with absolute joy. I imagined they watched as I had, with a mixture of laughter and tears.

I learned that one of the murdered athletes, Ze'ev Friedman, had sent a postcard to his parents from Munich before the attack. It arrived in their mailbox days after his death, their grief unbearable. Had their fingers touched the dried ink of his words knowing he was not coming home?

Munich 1972 and Beyond: The iconic image of the terrorist wearing a mask peering over the balcony also appeared several times in the documentary. An image that probably appeared on the anniversary of the massacre for over forty-five years. Ankie may have looked at it multiple times, coming face-to-face with the masked terrorist. The author of an invisible fate focused on destroying my love of the Games, an image that was prominent in our collective memory of the massacre.

Ankie's story: journalist, mother of a baby daughter, grief-stricken, and enraged by the reluctance of the IOC to recognize the murdered Israelis. And in an astonishing moment, she also revealed that since 1972, she had attended the opening ceremonies of every Olympics. Why would she subject herself to living so close to the memory of her husband's murder?

To never forget, was what she said; to educate, so that it never happens again. It was a sickening hope. By the time I watched the documentary, the world had already seen multiple acts of terrorism: terroristsm, motivated by anger that North Korea would not be given a chance to host the 1988 Games, had sent bombers who successfully downed a Korean airplane killing 115; then a domestic terrorist, protesting the spirit of the Games in Atlanta in 1996, injuring many and leaving a child motherless; and then the fifty citizens killed in the London bombings in 2005 after their city had been named the host for the 2012 Games. In total, over the twentieth century, forty-two Olympians and Paralympians and hundreds of spectators have died. It is as if the rituals of the Games had provided a global script for terror and murder, and not a place of peace, not a village with no borders.

And yet, '*do not forget...to educate*'—Ankie said several more times. She had conviction and determination; she had never stopped believing in the power of Olympism.

Munich 1972 and Beyond: Ankie saw her husband for the last time as he stood at the window of 31 Connollystrasse. He looked like a scholar with his black rimmed glasses. He spoke both German and English, negotiating with German officials on behalf of the terrorists through a second-floor window. How was the treatment of the hostages? 'Well, all, but one,' he answered. By then that one, Yossef Romano, a burly weightlifter, had been shot twice and castrated, left to bleed to death while the other Israeli hostages, dressed in their underwear, hands tightly bound behind their back, watched. The conversation ended as Andrei was hit with the butt of a rifle.

The orangeness of the family room closed in as I watched the footage of Andrei at the window. Athletes I had traveled with to Germany, chosen to compete in the Games, lived in dorms close to the hostage-taking. Had they heard the shots the night the hostages were taken? Did they know the Israeli woman sprinter whose coach was about to be murdered? Were they safe? How were they living with the horror? Were they shattered, broken? I still imagine the worst; I have never heard their stories of that day.

And then the afternoon after the hostage-taking. I am standing in my bedroom with my running gear laid out on my bed, moving in slow motion. I was probably late so I would have changed and hurried out the door, furiously riding my bike back to school. No Churchill Drive. Instead, we might have practiced at the school track. It was near a newly constructed four-lane highway. Cars would be buzzing. The day was sunny with big fluffy clouds that rolled and tumbled as they rearranged themselves, first a chariot, then a marshmallow, and then an arc of white dust. I remember the roar of a diesel engine bus mingling with shame. I like to think that we did not practice that day. It would have been as if the hostages, fellow athletes with Olympic dreams, were not our concern. When I try to remember what I did that day, I can only see the iconic image of the terrorist on the balcony, leaning over the edge, his finger so comfortable on the trigger of his automatic weapon.

Maybe I never went to that practice.

Everything about those days was familiar, and yet everything forever mis-remembered.

Munich 1972 and Beyond: Eighteen hours after the hostages were taken, it is reported that a settlement had been reached to free the hostages. A large bus appeared on the TV screen, rolling into the underground parking lot of the apartment building where the hostages and terrorists were staying. The image is dark and grainy, but I can see the outlines of the hostages roped together slowly making their way into the bus. Had they felt the possibility of stumbling? Each athlete appeared to step carefully so as to not pull their teammate to the ground. They were minutes away from death, surrendering their athletic selves as they concentrated on halting baby steps, helping their fellow man, avoiding a perilous fall.

That was a courageous act worthy of an Olympic hero.

I wondered if the terrorists saw the same courage that I saw. Had they begun to doubt their resolve in the face of the careful steps of athletic bodies? Or were they rationalizing their actions?

The Palestinian journalists interviewed in the documentary told their side of the story.

They viewed the Israeli athletes as soldiers, now considered to be prisoners of war, to be held in Cairo until a prisoner exchange could be arranged. Soldiers disguised as athletes, they rationalized. How could we be surprised that soldiers had been captured?

There was no war that day in Munich. It was just athletes looking forward to competing, to-be-the-best-they-could-be. There had been music festivals and comradery, no borders. I had seen it on TV in the early days of the Munich Games. It had been a story that had fired up my own desire to pursue my Olympic dreams. How had that sentiment, the wonder of Olympism, not been a part of the terrorist's calculation?

Or maybe it was. Because it was the Games, the slaughtering of innocence their goal—it would have a global audience. There were no images of the terrorists getting onto the bus, their body language cloaked in darkness. Still, it seemed impossible that they did not see what I saw. They must have and somewhere in the recesses of their minds, they must have realized that the athletes, who they were about to massacre, were just that, athletes, passionate about sport, not soldiers.

The doors shut, but the bus waits for minutes and then slowly begins to roll, slipping away into the darkness. The sound of military helicopters hovered. Ankie tells us that the bus was on its way to nearby Fürstenfeldbruck, a NATO airbase. She too had watched the bus, the athletes roped together and then the bus fading into a black night. She was with her father and the other families of the hostages. They have already learned that the German police have negotiated secure flights to Cairo for the terrorists in exchange for the hostages' freedom. She has doubts. And then a truth grabs hold.

The sound of the helicopters flutter overhead and then fades away. Everything in that moment is slipping out of reach, a moment that feels like she never again will see Andrei alive. Helicopter sounds would haunt Ankie for the rest of her life.

The world waits. We hear that there has been a fire fight and explosions at the airport. Ankie calls German officials, repeatedly. The news goes from bad to worse. A few have been injured, some have been killed, and then on the TV screen at three twenty-four in the morning on September 6th, Jim McKay appears. He begins to speak remembering the words of his father, "our greatest hopes and worst fears are seldom realized. Our worst fears have been realized." McKay stops talking. His eyes look directly into the camera. His golden yellow jacket seems out of place. An unusual color, possibly designed to underscore the golden moments of sports drama, the gold medal of Olympic heroes? He returned his gaze to his papers as if searching for answers, a nervous, grief-stricken body adorned in gold, steely in its determination to not display the pain of grief.

"…eleven hostages; two were killed in their rooms yesterday morning, nine were killed at the airport, tonight, they are gone, they are all gone…"

The next shot is of Ankie talking to the camera. Her face undisturbed, except a quivering right eye. A shaky but brief pause.

There were eight terrorists. Five were dead. The three survivors would be arrested and then let free five months later, as part of the negotiations for the release of passengers of a hijacked Lufthansa plane. Two of the three terrorists were reportedly assassinated by the Mossad over the next decades. The third, has spent his years in hiding, but was once interviewed by a Palestinian journalist, declaring that, "Before Munich, the world had no idea about the Palestine struggle, but on that day, the name of 'Palestine' was repeated all around the world."

In response to the massacre, Israel bombed ten PLO bases in Syria and Lebanon killing 200 militants and 11 civilians. It is also true that some of the massacred Israeli athletes had fought in the military. Conflict born of the horror of prior world wars, a cycle of hate propelling revenge and violence that now had embraced the Games.

McKay's final words fell out of the TV and collided with my body that had spent hours hoping, maybe even praying, that a happy ending was at hand. My mother sat on a couch clutching her purse and then rummaging inside it and pulling out a cigarette. She lit the cigarette and blew the smoke into the room, even though months ago she had proclaimed she had given up smoking. My father leaned back into his chair and swatted the smoke away. His face cracked into a jagged frown, a strike of disbelief. Tears. I was certain he was crying. I had never seen him cry.

I tried to blink it all away, again and again, with each *'all gone'* that McKay spoke, I began to understand that the word *gone* meant *dead*. Athletes were dead, murdered in plain sight. In 1972, I had never known anyone in my family or my friends' families or the athletes I trained with, to die. I had known only the assassination of leaders, like the Kennedys, or Martin Luther King. The Israeli's were just athletes, some were students, they were fathers with small children. They were just human beings who wanted to compete, to be the best-that-they-could-be.

My father came and sat cross-legged on the floor beside me. His hand floated up into the air, hesitant of where to land, his fingers scissoring, wavering, finally coming to rest on my shoulder. Fear mingled with uncertainty. Everything becomes unhinged.

"Don't worry," he said, "It'll be okay." His voice wavered. For the first time in my life, I knew his common sense was wrong-headed.

For the next few nights, sitting in front of TV tables pushing food around our soggy tin foil plates, we watched the continuing coverage of the massacre always with the backdrop of the image of the terrorist on the balcony, again and again he appeared.

"Terrorists win if they cancel the Games," proclaimed my father.

"I hope…" My mother's voice trailed away while another cigarette teetered. "So courageous…" as if she worried that another attack would surely come.

Protests against continuing the Games emerged. It felt as though the world would not survive.

Munich 1972 and Beyond: The documentary told yet another story. After the massacre, Ankie returned to 31 Connollystrasse, to the room where her husband spent his last days. The documentary shows the chaos: feces, bullet holes in the wall, clothing, and a body's worth of dried blood. On her way in and out, other athletes scurry to and from training sessions. Eleven people murdered and the mantra, the Games must go on, seems out of place. I wondered, *did anybody really believe that?* Among those murdered at the airport was a German police officer. I wondered what his family believed.

Shocking newspaper headlines descended. 'Massacre at Munich: Will the Games Go On?'

A German headline, more certain: 'Games end in Tragedy: Continuing the Games is like holding a dance at Dachau.'

In the end, the Games continued, and the crowds came and cheered. I watched, dumbfounded by just how normal the competitions had become, half expecting that another hostage-taking was imminent. My father had resumed watching, but his body language revealed defeat. My mother smoked cigarette after cigarette, the smoke curling around her head, as she stiffened when the iconic image of the terrorist would pop up on the TV.

Years later, I would discover that the Egyptian team, fearing reprisals, left the Munich Games and did not compete. Also, Dutch athlete Jos Hermens, the world record holder in the 5000 meters, even before it had been known that the Games would continue, announced that he was not going to compete: *'The happy games are no more, athletes have been killed.'*

The story goes that Avery Brundage, the president of the IOC, had insisted that the Games go on. Did the Olympians want to compete? If it had been me, would I have wanted the Games to continue? But how, I wondered, amidst all that sorrow and disbelief, was it not the end of the Games? How could anyone muster the energy to compete, to care about winning?

Munich 1972 and Beyond: The documentary compiled a montage of the news coverage—the faces of journalists and officials, showing the hints of hope at the beginning of the hostage taking that fell into despair as the massacre played out, who now trained their words and images on the memorial that German officials had arranged for the day after the airport massacre. Collectively, they felt certain that the Games would *not* continue.

The camera spans the crowd of athletes on the infield of the stadium, and the spectators taking a seat, I remember seeing them sweaty, worn down. I remember thinking it must have been terribly humid. The Games could not possibly continue.

The funeral march from Beethoven's symphony '*Eroica,*' an ode to sorrow, began. I knew how to play it on the piano. I stared at my fingers, alternating between clenching and trembling. I wonder how the musicians found the courage to play, it took every ounce of strength I had not to cry in front of my parents—such an emotion had been declared as a version of '*getting too carried away.*' Tears were something now relegated to our bedrooms, tears soaking into the pillow. Or in my case, my tattered childhood pink poodle.

Violins begin their mournful beat. Athletes in the center of the field, either stand and sway or sit on lopsided folding chairs. They look like as if they are holding their breath. I think I can see soldiers' fan out from the cauldron that held the Olympic flame, still belching up and out. Their guns appear to be held at eye level ready to shoot.

The French horns of the orchestra joined the violins. An honor guard of the Munich Police, in blue dress uniforms, march out from the stadium tunnel and take their place alongside the athletes. Their blue uniforms and the big blue sky collaborate in grief.

I am certain that the Games will not continue.

The speeches ring out as the cameras wander.

"The Games must go on…We declare today a day of mourning… continue… all events one day later than scheduled."

Absolute disbelief stunned us all into silence. Spectators dab their eyes, lower their heads, tears, and then images of eleven coffins draped in the flag of Israel. The Israeli athletes are dressed in their country's traditional blue and white uniform which matched the flag draped coffins. It seems as though everyone is struggling to hold back their tears, as if crying, even at this moment, is not what a strong Olympian would do.

It is an unbearable spectacle—athletes that believed in athleticism, the bonds it forged, had been murdered because of the politics of hate. The television screen did not lie; we were all living drenched in agony.

"The Olympic ideals live on. In the events we have lived through, there is no line dividing North from South, East from West. Where the break comes, it is between the brotherhood of all men who wish for peace, and hatred of those who expose the worst… dangers against the values that make life worth living."

Peace is what makes life worth living.

Years later, when asked, the families of the slain athletes would say that their loved ones would have wanted the Games to continue. How and why athletes made that decision remains an untold story. But one athlete who did compete after the memorial tells yet another tale of agony.

Canadian members of the water polo team were at the chain link fence the night of the hostage taking. They had helped the terrorists, dressed as athletes with heavy gun toting gym bags, climb over the fence to get into the village. They assumed the terrorists were athletes like them, sneaking back to the dorms after watching the Canada-Soviet hockey final at the media center. Canada had won the game. They were happy, drunk on nationalism.

After the massacre, the team competed in their competitions. Decades later, after the story had been told and retold that it was American athletes that had helped the terrorists over the fence, one of the Canadian swimmers eventually told the true story as he stood in front of a classroom full of grade school children. A question innocently asked by a student arose unexpectedly. Catching the Olympic swimmer off guard. What did he know about the massacre? With one foot in the past, and the other in front of all those innocent faces, he broke down in tears. The story of helping the terrorists unfolded, an untold story that had worked its way to the tip of his tongue.

The dramatic image of the masked terrorist was shown many times in the years between 1972 and the London Games of 2012—an image of Black September lording over the Games. By now I had seen it so many times and noticed that atop the mask there was a woolly, matted blob. I imagined that in his hurry to terrorize he had put his mask on inside out.

The London Opening Ceremonies were scheduled to be held on the 40th anniversary of the massacre. Ankie Spitzer and other families of the murdered athletes were calling for a moment of silence, or rather had been calling for some recognition of the murdered athletes and the policeman in the ten intervening Games; the IOC had refused, once defending their decision as a way to avoid a round of boycotts by Arab nations.

"Let them leave if they can't understand what the Olympics are all about—a connection between people through sport," was Ankie's retort. The night of London's Opening Ceremonies, NBC sportscaster, Bob Costas, commented on the tragedy of IOC's refusal, "many people find that denial more than puzzling."

Rabbi Joseph Potasnik, a rabbi, radio host, and executive vice president of the New York Board of Rabbis, said, "37,360...the number of minutes in the entire Olympics and they [couldn't] find one."

Jibril Rajoub, president of the Palestine Olympic Committee was thankful for the IOC's refusal, noting that sports for Palestinians were, "...a bridge to love, interconnection, and spreading of peace among nations."

But the most telling were from family members of the murdered athletes: Barbara Berger, whose brother David was killed in the massacre wrote:

> 'A moment of silence, a formal recognition of this horrific tragedy may not seem like much...this would not just be a memorial for Israel; it would be a memorial for all Olympians. Our children and brothers, the Munich 11, were not only children of Israel, but children of the Olympics. They embodied the Olympic spirit of teamwork and community, of honest competition and our common humanity. They were integral embers in the flame of the Olympic torch. They were killed only because of who they were: Jews, Israelis, champions of the Jewish state.'

Ankie had been relentless in her pursuit of Olympic officials. Every Games she made the request, the organizing committees responded with the weirdly historical refrain of Coubertin: the Games, specifically the Opening Ceremonies, were to be free from politics. It was clear to journalists and historians and almost everyone else on earth that the Games had never been free from politics, and would never be free from revenge fueled by hate.

Ankie eventually found a way, one she dares not reveal in the documentary, to have official documents from the German police investigations of the massacre released. The most horrific were the 900 forensic photos both in the village and at the airfield where the gun battle was held. There were images of the burned bodies; of the hostages' hands still bound behind their backs; their bodies riddled with bullet holes. There had been confusion. A gun battle; then a fire started as the terrorists lobbed hand grenades into the helicopters. I prayed that the athletes were dead from the bullets long before the ball of fire consumed them.

Finally, by 2016, Thomas Bach, president of the IOC since 2013—who won a gold medal at the 1976 Games in Montreal as a fencer—who may have felt some allegiance to Ankie's husband's sport, agreed to honor the dead athletes at a ceremony in the Rio Olympic Village. He noted that fifteen athletes had died at the Olympics since 1896, eleven from the Munich massacre. Shortly thereafter, donations from government and private sources increased to build a memorial to the murdered athletes and policeman.

Munich 1972 and Beyond: The documentary showed clips of German government officials involved with the building of the memorial near the site of the Olympic village. It rests unassumingly along a quiet walking path in Munich's Olympic Park. Visitors to the site descend a short set of steps to enter the main space, which looks like a sanctuary. The large exhibition area is set in the back and seems almost like a cave, resting under a thick mound of grass and blending into a backdrop of Linden trees. Along the back wall, a large LED screen plays a 27-minute loop of news footage broadcast during the crisis. In the center of the memorial, a triangular column displayed the biographical profiles of each victim in German and English, with photographs.

On the day of the memorial's dedication, Werner Karg, an official in the Bavarian Ministry of Culture, spoke, "The Munich massacre is remembered by the haunting images of masked terrorists. We need to also see the faces of the victims. We can show that these were individuals, ordinary people, not just names."

Forty-seven years later, the public would become familiar with the lives of the Israeli athletes, would hear about their hopes and dreams, and meet the families that had carried on in the aftermath of the massacre. Added to the agony of grief would be the sense of shame that it had taken so long to face the truth.

However, it was Ankie's story about the Atlanta Games in 1996 that lifted the burden of unbearable agony and shame. Between 1972 and 1996, twenty-four years, the age of her daughter, Ankie found the voice of her husband's legacy.

By 1996, she had decided to bring the adult children of the slain athletes, including her daughter, to the Atlanta Games. It was the first Olympics to employ artistic designers to use technology to brand a mascot. It looked like a tear drop with feet and oversized facial features. Coincidentally, Atlanta was the first Games where Palestine would be allowed to send athletes. A concession negotiated during Peace talks led by President Carter.

Ankie's face shifts into another gear. "I asked my children what they would do when the Palestinians walked into the stadium."

"My children said, 'They are athletes…we are going to applaud them too. They are not responsible for what happened in Munich…these athletes would have been friends of our fathers.'"

Ankie hesitates, a flicker of grief, a brisk blink, a pause, the longest she has allowed since the documentary began.

It's a moment of absolute hope. A fusion of what everyone had said, even the Arab Olympic officials, "Sport was a bridge…to love, interconnection, and spreading of peace among nations."

It is a pause where you could rest from the unbearable. What would Palestinian athletes say? They too had lost family members in the aftermath of the massacre.

There is no answer.

"I had taught them not to hate." She was referring to the children who were forced to grow up in a fatherless world.

Spitzer speaks her next words with a breathless clarity— sadness and truth mingle. It feels like absolute wisdom, a tsunami of fresh air.

"I taught them not to hate."

A deep sigh, a gasp, a crisp, clean breath, and another pause, filled with words that echoed…*not to hate, I taught them not to hate*…and then again…*not to hate.*

Ankie returned to the Games for so many years, living the words of her husband, standing by the dreams of Coubertin's Olympism, even when so much had been taken from her, her daughter, and from the families of the massacred. Athleticism and the dreams of athletes for two weeks every four years had found a common ground in the rituals of the Opening Ceremonies—a time and place it seems, where there had been peace, the legacy of the murdered athletes, not to hate.

"It was the Olympics, there are no borders."

For all the stories of the Games, this is the story that tells the essential meaning of sport. It means something. It should be told and retold, a timeless rendering that gives the culture of athleticism a loud, proud, heroic voice. To teach children not to hate—no matter the cost—is rooted in Coubertin's Olympism, a belief that Ankie Spitzer kept alive. It is the story embedded in the Munich memorial—we must not and cannot look away. For this one time, do not look away.

More importantly, this is the true legacy of Andrei Spitzer, the Israeli athletes, and the German police officer who died that day, not the iconic image of the terrorist, embracing an automatic weapon while wearing an inside out woolly mask.

CHAPTER FIFTEEN

Gerard Mach: "To be the Slowest to Slow Down."

"The important thing is to not stop questioning.
Curiosity has its own reason for existing."
Albert Einstein

I'm sure it was a Sunday afternoon in the winter of 1973, but this time we were at the University's '*Gritty Grotto,*' the basement of the physical education building at the University of Manitoba campus on the southern outskirts of Winnipeg. The asphalt running surface, about three to four feet wide, and built as an afterthought, wound its way around cement pillars and piles of dirt. At one end was a straight away that intersected the sort-of-middle of the irregular-shaped running track. It was here where we could set up our blocks and practice starts, run wind sprints, and stretch.

Dust and the smell of sweat clogged the air; the ceiling was comically low.

But I overlooked the absurdity of the grotto, a place that had the gift of changing rooms and showers so we could change into dry clothes for the frosty drive home. I had access to the whirlpool and the physiotherapist. A place that met my father's common sense ideas and above all else, it felt like the best place for an athlete, especially one with achy muscles. A sense that now accompanied many of my workouts.

That Sunday was the day I first met Gerard Mach. The week before had been filled with facts about his story: hired to be the Canadian National Sprint Coach touring the country to meet sprinters and their coaches, and curiously, a coach who was on loan from Poland. I'm sure they told us that Mach had coached Irena Szewinska, considered one of the best woman sprinters of all time, who at one time held world records in the 100-, 200-, and 400-meter sprints, winning seven medals (three golds over four Olympic Games). Munich 1972 was her last, winning a bronze in the 200- meters.

I wondered if he had been in Munich to see Szewinska's final victory. What had he seen and thought about the massacre? We were also told that it was in Munich where Adidas, the name we had given our spikes, had arranged for a meeting between Mach and Canadian track and field officials. It was at that meeting where he had been invited to come to Canada. It was fitting that our shoes and Mach had some magical connection.

I was struck with amazement over the fact that a coach could be loaned to us. I assumed it was to prepare us Olympic hopefuls for the Montreal Games. Winning medals for the nation as the Canadian flag and anthem soared. Why did Poland not want more medals for their sprinters? Why loan their competitors, their successful all-knowing coach? The question hovered and then fell off the radar screen. Indeed, Mach never returned to Poland, living the rest of his life in Canada. His family joined him sometime in the next decade, and they settled in Vancouver, the destination of my family's failed car trips.

Mach was short and a bit chubby. That first day he wore a gray track jacket and pants, light in color. He had a mischievous smile and eyes that danced along with a mutton-chop-styled beard. When he spoke, he had a thick accent, and yet he made himself understood. I had heard others characterize him as simple-minded, naive, perhaps because his English was a second language, or maybe his third or fourth. It seemed to me that he chose his words carefully, chewing on their articulation with his bushy jowls. And as it turned out for me, his words shaped not only my athleticism, but would, from time to time, echo between my athletic past and my adult future. He understood the story of the interlocking parts of anatomy and physiology, and I understood that he had a lot to teach me about sprinting.

I'm sure we jogged and then stretched close to where the starting blocks were. My coach stood off to the side, leaning on his canes, towering over Mach in a friendly way. Explaining that as a child he had polio, left with two shriveled legs. Canes and braces, he said, necessary for him to walk. Mach looked troubled, but then with a deepening smile he shook the hand of my coach. I assumed that suffering through war and polio provided a common understanding, even though Mach, at times, also appeared puzzled by my coach's corny clichés. He nodded as if stashing them away for further study.

I felt butterflies in my tummy as I peeked at the two men and tried to do a decent job of warming up for the workout. I wanted to make a good impression. I spent a long time doing stretching exercises, longer than usual, only to discover that my achiness was dissolving into the gently held muscle tugs, a release that cascaded throughout my body. I felt ready to make a good impression.

Our coach proudly introduced us, including our best times over 100-meters. He then motioned us over to the straightaway inside of the asphalt track so that we would not be interrupted by the other runners.

"I teach to you the ABCs of sprinting," Mach said.

The 'A' was a type of marching: thigh lift, light footfall, arms and upper body loose, but not lazy. We did several repetitions covering only five meters. Then another five reps over ten meters, and then another five reps over ten meters but, at the end, we were to break from the 'A' configuration into a light relaxed running form. The tappity-tap of our feet fell into a rhythm. I felt a warmth building from the inside out wringing out the last threads of achiness .

The 'B' drill was next, covering the same ten meters, but this time lifting the knee and extending the foreleg, goose-stepping. I could feel my quads working hard as my feet slapped the ground, a hard stop that was not painful. Out of the corner of my eye I saw Mach nodding his approval.

The 'C' drill once more covered the same distance, but this time Mach wanted us to lift a straight leg, no knee bending, up and down, landing on my forefoot and then leveraging my body forward. It felt familiar, toe-walking that controlled my nervous energy. My whole world clicked into place. The give and take of thigh muscles, an urge to gallop forward spiraled up, down and then outward, from the ground up. The teachings of Mach resonated with everything I had felt as a toe-walker, a toe-runner, and now a sprinter.

It was brilliant, a set of drills that strengthened muscles, not measured by pounds lifted, but with an upright posture, a balanced arm swing, slow meticulous movements that laid down the perceptions of power and speed, forming an unconscious muscle memory of perfect form.

"A is for thigh lift, B is for knee extension, and C is for hip extension," my coach summarized, but I knew he had failed to understand their true purpose.

We must have done other things that day, but we ended up practicing starts. Mach explained the biomechanics of it, how sprinting was about attaining top speed, at first driving out of the blocks and then slowly rising as our legs unleashed their power. Slowly rising was important. And then moving erect, body tall and relaxed, no head wagging, no scrunching the shoulders or face grimacing, just letting go and feeling the power surge. Let the acceleration emerge, hitting top speed at about sixty meters. Then, he said, as if he had become one of us—"*We* were to hold on."

He pointed at me. "To win, the sprinter must be the slowest to slow down."

Effortlessness and winning. It was a defining moment.

Curiosity was something my family never talked about at dinnertime but rather, something that we did. Never once doubting its grip on me, my parents had underscored common sense with curiosity.

I discovered it on laundry days. On those days my mother and I explored the blond-covered cedar chest nestled in the cool basement while she banged and swore and prodded the wringer washing machine. Each artifact I found prompted a story from my mother: the story of her wedding day as my hand cradled her silky wedding dress, of Kenora where they had honeymooned, of its preceding adventurous train ride one of the first times she had been outside of Winnipeg. Then the sad stories of how her father died suddenly of a heart attack, of how she had to quit school which was the reason why I had to graduate from university.

She had learned how to write shorthand. I studied her slim yellowed schoolbook, pages worn, pencil markings in the margin where she had practiced squiggles intermingled with arithmetic. Her favorite thing in the world, to sum, subtract, divide, and multiply. Curiosity wrapped up with good sense.

Memories had found their footing: wrapped in the veil of silk dresses, cuddled by the sweet smell of her schoolbook, and decorated by the flecks of gold that fell from the pages of the Encyclopedia Britannica; to which I added the rhythmical words of Mach—"to be the slowest to slow down."

A curious phrase, long-limbed words as if the joy of effortlessness was yoked to motivation. Athleticism was not a grinding grunt, it was a letting go, it was soaring with joy, it was holding on. It was the secret that defined Olympic excellence.

CHAPTER SIXTEEN

Overtraining

"We cannot solve our problems with the same thinking we
used when we created them."
Albert Einstein

After my humiliation in the international competitions,
I narrowed my sights to what I had to do to make the
Olympic team for Montreal. I figured I had been noticed and
if I returned the following season, faster than ever, it would
erase the memory of my poor showing. The Canadian Track
and Field association had given me the 'C' ranking. I reasoned
that they were willing to take a chance that I might rise to the
occasion for Montreal.

During that winter—nine months of below-zero
weather—training indoors was the only option. Mostly I ran
in the basement of the new physical education building at the
University, but on Sundays, I ran in my coach's apartment
stairway, twelve flights of stairs, two at a time followed by
a small rest during the elevator ride down to the basement.
By the third repetition, my breathing hurt more than my legs,
which was surprising, given the forces my muscles were
producing absorbed by the surface of joints and the tautness of

ligaments. But I blindly trusted my coach's wisdom. This was how I was going to win. The thigh lift: it gave me an edge, a longer stride, that meant more soaring, more distance covered in the fastest time.

One Sunday the elevator ride down to the basement slowed. A physician hurriedly walked through the folding doors, a stethoscope peeking from a large leather purse that was tucked under her arm.

As the doctor registered my flushed face and breathlessness, she seemed more alarmed than surprised. My coach squirmed. She ignored him and looked at me. "I'm a doctor," her forehead now frowning, "…uhm, are you alright?"

My coach answered, "We're okay."

His thick body towered over us despite the fact that he leaned heavily on two canes. It was an odd few seconds. I think I saw his face turn a light shade of red, embarrassment, contrary to what I knew him to be. He was a man of clichés, littering his commentary with stock phrases and a booming authority. I had never seen him embarrassed about anything.

"No-pain-no-gain," he said and then expounded on his training philosophy: general fitness in the fall, endurance and stair running in the winter.

The elevator descended to the main floor. My head began to pound. The doctor gestured with disbelief, a slow swivel of her head from side to side. Looking at him and then me, she tells us that the stairwell's ventilation is connected to the underground parking lot which means that as I run the stairs, I am breathing in carbon monoxide. And then she adds with a stern doctorly voice…not a good thing.

Later, at Sunday dinner, my father and I talked about my stair running. He wondered if this punishing workout was healthy, especially for a girl's body. I told him how my breathing became unusually hard probably due to the carbon monoxide that drifted into the stairwell. He stopped short of telling me that my coach was wrong. He too just shook his head. He didn't say it, but I know he was thinking it. Stair running did not make sense.

Later that year, Gerard Mach, now firmly acknowledged as the Canadian national sprint coach, singled out my thigh lift as the best in the nation. "Stair running," my coach said boastfully, leaving out the story of the carbon monoxide.

I did not know then that a high thigh lift was an impressive accomplishment. A successful form for an Olympic hopeful. What I did know was that it was a comment from the coach who would have an opinion on who was to be chosen to be a member of the women's sprint relay team for the Montreal Games. What I did notice was that he had noticed me. Stair running gained a revered honorary status over common sense.

It was the first day of Spring, the outdoor high school track season loomed, my last as a high school senior, but it was still too cold to train outside. After classes, we jogged in the deserted hallways warming our bodies, stretching muscles, and then adding the prescribed set of Mach's sprinting drills. We bantered back and forth as each of us tried to remember Mach's exact words. The drills were effortless, and our coach hurried us to pay attention to the workout. He had already said that he thought Mach's ideas were frivolous, of secondary importance compared to the times he recorded on his stopwatch.

The school team, both boys and girls, trained together on that day. Our coach's habit was to inject some competitiveness into the workout. He started with a discussion of form and technique for coming out of the starting blocks. He used the boys as an example and pointed to the zig-zag of my start as the incorrect way, and then to add to the spirit of it all, he paired me with the boys directing us to race the length of the hallway. He sat in a folding chair, called the commands, and then slapped his hands to mimic the sound of the starter's pistol. In our heads we were competing, but in reality, we were play-acting, pretending that we did not care to win.

I cared. After all, there was a delicious thought that I could beat a boy, especially with an adrenalin rush, like a real competition, I felt the adrenaline rush. My body took the challenge personally, every joint and muscle on alert. I had beaten the boys before, but lately, they had been getting faster, much faster. I wanted to beat them again, the best thigh lift in the nation was at stake.

I crouched down onto all fours beside a boy, who was younger than me. He had told me he wanted to play football, a running back. Earlier that year, another teacher, who also played for the local professional football team (the Winnipeg Blue Bombers), had told us that my time over 40 yards was faster than his burly teammates. The scene was set. If football was in my teammate's future, he had to win this race.

"Get set!" the coach yelled.

Butts in the air.

Smack!

I flinched at the sound of the clap rather than a real pistol. Bursting forward arms pumping, leaning, and then rising up. Behind. His start had been faster.

Each of my thighs lifted and then my lower leg straightened, a swift unfolding, a footfall and push-off.

But with each contact there was a slip of my forefoot.

Shiny linoleum tiles, probably newly polished, covered the cement hallway floor.

A familiar acceleration, power rising, hitting top speed. Closing in, coming even. I squeezed out one more ounce of effort.

A bigger slippage.

And then my hamstring twisted, a stiffening resistance followed by a sharp pain, deep in the center of my muscle belly and then rippling out, and downward, a slicing pain as if the sharp edge of a knife was gliding through raw meat.

I slipped, covering inches of linoleum in seconds, but then abruptly slowed, coming to a stop while at the same time grabbing the back of my thigh. My left hand, twisting my body to reach the pain. An egg-sized ball of skin, pushed by fibrillating muscle, filled the palm of my hand.

Torn hamstring, a deep tear, the physio would tell me later, but there had not been the sound of the pop, so everything was probably still attached.

"You're lucky," he said, "I've seen worse."

Afterward, I remembered how my walking changed, the pain of the muscle, when and where it occurred, it embedded itself into each step. Short or long, fast or slow. Almost immediately uncertainty surrounded how I should train with a severe but not the worse kind of torn hamstring. My father wondered if I should run at all.

I assumed that the swelling would subside as I went from walking to jogging. Eventually that became pain free. But not totally. It was as if I had a third eye surveying the very spot where the muscle had torn, now vulnerable with every movement. Within a month or so I was running fast, the muscle was stiff and sore, but not painful. And then sprinting, where the pain had turned into an ache, a tug with every thigh lift, easy to ignore.

"Try running at half speed," my coach said, "Pain?" he would ask. If yes, then it would be "…well… try half of half speed." It was a trial-and-error approach.

I saw the physiotherapist at the University along with many other student athletes, all of us with some sort of injury. Sometimes he was available before a workout, sometimes after. In either case, I would get into the whirlpool for fifteen minutes and then he would massage the muscle.

Maybe he also showed me some stretching exercises. Probably hurdle stretches—sitting on the floor, one leg straight, one leg bent so that its foot touched the inner thigh of the straight leg. Lean forward nose over my kneecap, stretch to the point of pain, back off, hold the stretch—no bouncing, count to thirty.

By bending one leg, I released the muscles of my low back so that I could stretch the muscle of my straightened leg. The therapist told me I was tight: tight low back, thigh muscles, hamstrings, and gastrocs. By now I knew this was short for the two heads of the gastrocnemius muscle and the soleus, a powerful multipennate muscle that lay beneath the gastroc. Because the gastrocnemius, from its origin at the heel bone to its insertion behind the knee, crossed two joints, I had to stretch two different ways. Once with my knee straight and then with it bent. I loved this stretch, a momentary distraction from my torn hamstring, releasing the ache that spread from my heel bone to my low back. The physio's knowhow had unlocked the tightness unleashing a muscle sense that I had never felt before.

The therapist also commented on my ankles, amazed at their unusual stiffness, at how the arch of my foot was high—supinated—he said, a term I did not know, but sounded like a word that a physiotherapist should know. From my butt to my toes, my legs were permanently fashioned to hit the ground running, to leverage my body forward, to power my sprint. I had the perfect alignment of muscle, leg and foot bones that created a powerful force but that had tightened my hamstrings. Pulling a hamstring muscle was a matter of when, not if, especially after I had perfected the thigh lift with the stair running workouts.

Pain soon dissolved into tugging as if the torn muscle was a thick wad of taffy. When I poked at the spot where the ball had originally formed it hardened. The physio's massaging fingers, fists, and his pointy elbow worked over the muscle as if it were a cold ball of clay that he could refashion into a strong but pliable piece of meat. Some days he made it hurt more than the workout, some days he took away the ache.

Stretching before and after workouts was becoming a ritual that I needed to follow as if it were my religion, no shortcuts. It would be the only way I could sprint again. It was the only way I could manage the achiness that was taking over my body—ankles and hamstrings, my low back, and the balls of my feet. I had often shunned the ritual of a warm-up, but now it was as necessary as breathing.

Visits to the physiotherapist soon became a luxury.
That fall I started university at the School of Rehabilitation
Medicine, eight hours of classes, five days a week. After class
I drove to the arena for a workout, and then back to the school
library to study. The college and library were midway between
the arena and my parent's house where I still lived. Going
to the university campus to train and get a massage from the
physiotherapist was never going to happen. The campus was on
the city's outskirts, at least an hour's car ride, time that I needed
to study.

Most days I arrived at the library in my stinky track
clothes covered in nylon pants that made a swishing sound
when I walked, breaking the silence for the other students that
were already hunkered down in their books. I garnered stern
looks, mocking my unusual appearance. Eventually, when I
came into the library, I headed for the nearest available study
carrel. I remember feeling like I did not fit in, a noisy oddball
student, not the studious quiet type.

When I got home, my parents would serve up a cold
dinner, and sometimes talk about how unhealthy it was to go
out in the cold after sweating at practice. They repeated my
words about the cold and clammy ride, telling me that I would
soon 'catch a darn good cold,' which I dismissed as an old
wives' tale. It was common sense my father would say listing
the cause of my complaints: running on hard cement, exposing

a hot body to coldness, no wonder my knees were sore (one of my usual complaints).

Eventually I would see a physician about my knees. He wondered out loud if my training shoes that I had worn to the appointment, thick soles, and leather uppers, were too heavy. He theorized that as I swung my leg forward, I was straining my knee medial and lateral collateral ligaments (by now I had learned their correct anatomical names). He palpated my kneecaps and twisted each knee in several directions and pronounced everything taut, perfectly taut. But as he poked at the ligaments, I felt a bruising pain.

He hummed and hawed and finally asked me to flex and straighten my knee as he placed his hand over my kneecap.

"Your kneecap is very small for the size of your thigh bone." I stared at my knee and saw the triangular shaped bone, and it looked like it always had but it did seem small compared to the large ones I had seen in my anatomy classes. By the end of the visit, he had declared that his impression was that what I needed to do was isometric exercises.

At dinnertime, I told my father about the physician's verdict. He had gone to great lengths to find a physician with a reputation for common sense. I summed up my aches and pains, the hamstring, the knee ligaments, and my odd kneecaps. He thought the theory of heavy shoes made sense and decided to buy me a new lighter pair. He had found a secondhand set of weights I could use to do weight training in the basement behind family room, which included a weight boot. One hundred repetitions of small leg lifts. Contracting my quads with a straight leg while wearing the ten-pound boot, is what I had decided would suffice for isometric exercise. I did it every day for months.

The knee pain eventually went away, and I learned to live with the tug and ache of my hamstring. However, when I was home for dinner, usually Sunday dinner, there was still more talk about the cold weather, going from sweating to below-zero weather, about the relentless routine, classes, workout, and schoolwork. Was I keeping up with everything? My father would wonder out loud: *Were athletes not supposed to focus on healthy bodies?* Was mine becoming less healthy? My mother agreed with my father.

I remember his question but not my answer, probably because Gerard Mach had other ideas on how I was to return to elite competition, and I was thinking that my father would never understand Mach's new complicated ways, not examples of common sense. I assumed my father's high school education would not be good enough to understand the importance of muscle hypertrophy, or, the elegant give and take between hamstrings and quadriceps muscles. I probably said this in so many words, and he probably nodded.

Around this time, my father learned how to use the stopwatch. He wanted to volunteer as a timer at the local track meets. The sight of the smoke from the starter's pistol was the true start of the race, he told me—not the sound of the pistol's firing that ignited thrust from the blocks. As timers they were taught to focus on the smoke and not the sound.

Common sense as well as artistry, our common ground, merged with his curious role as a timekeeper. Our beliefs attended our dinnertime rituals, polite respectful storytelling, and yet the divide between my dreams and his common sense had taken root.

CHAPTER SEVENTEEN

The Junior Olympics: Edmonton, Alberta, August 1974

"[*The Games are*] more than pure entertainment, more than didactic or persuasive formulations, and more than cathartic indulgences. They are occasions in which as a culture or a society we repeat upon and define ourselves, dramatize our collective myths and history, present ourselves with alternatives, and eventually change in some ways while remaining the same in others."

J. J. MacAloon

On a hot summer day in August of 1974, I found myself baking in the treeless infield of the University of Alberta stadium. I'd been selected to be on the Manitoba Team that was to compete in a national junior track meet: an Olympic Exhibition. I felt the drops of sweat run down my face as I watched spectators fill the shaded stadium seating. Large banners announcing the Olympic backdrop to the meet flapped in the fiery hot breeze. It felt cringe-worthy. Being part of the Olympic movement was supposed to be meaningful, courageous, heroic; the whole idea of giving junior athletes a taste of the Olympic experience, as if you could practice winning a gold medal, was weird.

The 1976 Montreal Olympics were two years away, but they were on everybody's mind. The spectators strode to their seats with high expectations, gripped by the idea that the athletes competing in this exhibition were on the verge of being their home-grown Olympic heroes.

My parents were ecstatic that I had been invited to compete for the Manitoba team. We all considered, and by all, I mean local journalists as well as my aunts and uncles, that it meant I too could be part of the Games in Montreal.

I turned away from the spectators and began to survey the peaks of the nearby Rocky Mountains, snow-covered stony edifices that peeked over the edge of the stadium seating. Could there be a possibility of a cool breeze? Humid air pressed into my face. The ragweed pollen infiltrated my breath and eyes. Each breath on the verge of producing copious amounts of snot, while my gritty, red-rimmed eyes itched relentlessly. It felt like pain.

I joined up with my teammates. Our races were forty-five minutes away, twelve noon, right when the sun would beat down on the black asphalt track.

"Let's do three wind sprints and call it a day," I said, wishing to avoid the ABCs—a disruption in our usual pre-race routine—and yet it was an idea that popped out of my mouth without much thought. Besides the snot, my body was still reeling from the ache of the bus trip to Edmonton from Winnipeg—seventeen hours to cross the never-ending mid-western prairies and then another hour of stop and go before the driver found the location of the dorms.

I spied the arrival of my parents and watched as they found a shady spot to sit. They waved; I smiled and waved back. They had arrived by plane yesterday, an extravagance, but they had decided that they were too old for car trips. They were staying in a motor hotel near the airport. It was air conditioned, and the price of the room included a breakfast bun and coffee. They had plans to go out to a fancy restaurant with relatives.

Nothing like my dorm room: non-air-conditioned, small for two people, furnished with a desk and chair that separated two long twin beds. I was paired up with a sprinter from Saskatchewan, an attempt to encourage cross-cultural exchanges. We ate the usual cafeteria fare in large dining halls on the main floor. Mostly I was annoyed that my favorite pre-race food, peanut butter sandwiches and cool sweet lemonade, were nowhere to be found.

I decided on at least doing some wind sprints. Three. I started with a slow jog, an easy acceleration, and then a rapid-fire sprint. Hot air pushed against my face the faster I ran, burning the chapped raw skin around my nose. My eyes watered, a ticklish trickle that rolled down my face. It was clear that my allergy medications were *not* working.

"100-meter final to the starting line," called the marshal. I threw my racing shoes on the ground and watched as they landed with the spikes facing upwards. Four spikes on the soles of the shoes, thick and sharp, gleamed in the sunlight, eager to dig in.

I shrugged.

I sat down on the grassy infield for one last hamstring stretch, and did not pay attention to the distance between me and the shoes. I straightened my left limb and flexed the right one so that my lower leg folded back. It was what I called a two-fer stretch—hamstrings for the straight leg, quads for the bent one. I lowered my right knee to the ground. Not watching exactly where the knee would touch down. I closed my eyes, which was the cause of my problem, and gently pressed my lowering knee into one of the spikes of my running shoe. When I opened my eyes, surprised at the sensing of cool metal, I saw the spike sticking into the fleshy part of my quad just above my knee. No pain, just a squishy slick sound, something you would expect on a sweaty hot day.

"Final call–100-meters," an official called.

A jolt of adrenaline. I dislodged the spike from my knee and slipped the shoes on. Snot ran out of my nose. I wiped it away with a salty forearm and bent my knee to see the damage—a nail-sized hole, no bleeding, no pain, just a well-formed pit bounded by fleshy pink tissues, muscle, and a grisly white blob at its base, probably a ligament, maybe bone.

Time to run.

I felt the stares of the crowd. I had a pretty good idea what they were thinking—would this Manitoba girl be one of the few who would compete in Montreal?

I checked in with the marshal, discarded my track jacket and pants and practiced my starts. A small trickle of blood had started to run down my leg, I swiped at it, smearing it into a pale ribbon of red. The announcer called out our names, and then it was time, finally, to run the race.

The hot sun beat down on my back as I bent over and assumed the crouch position.

Bang!

My arms pumped, hot blood now flowing from my knee hole, and the usual soaring. The tiny spikes of my shoes dug in, unbounded power. I hit the 60-meter mark and automatically commanded my body to "be the slowest to slow down."
The finish line, the lean, and the deceleration—three of us crossed the line almost at the same time, one tenth of a second separating first from second and third. The scoreboard flashed our names, I had come in third.

Something that felt like relief descended along with a bout of non-stop sneezing.

The crowd cheered wildly, a muffled beat that matched the throbbing inside my head. I bent over to catch my breath; snot ran from my nose, and I spit the frothy slime onto the ground. A deep ache rose to the surface of the knee hole just as a bubble of blood burst through the tiny puncture and began to run down my leg. My hamstring was on fire.

I wandered over to my coach who was sitting in the shaded first row of seats, "Good enough," he said. I shrugged and began looking for a Kleenex, wondering what to wipe first, the blood on my shin, or the liquid snot leaking from my nose.

"Nothing horrible," he said, "Not your best, but you did nothing to make your chances worse."

The next day, after breakfast, we piled onto buses and assembled on the middle of the blazing hot field to the music of the university band for the closing ceremonies. The official speeches included words from Coubertin, *'swifter, higher, faster.'* Politicians touted their resolve to support athletes and hoped that this exhibition would inspire our dedication. Just imagine, representing your country, winning gold medals, singing the national anthem in your homeland. Glorious.

After the speeches we marched back to buses to be miraculously greeted by a wall of cool air. Someone had thought about air-conditioning. My body tried and failed to dissipate its heat. I imagined diving into a swimming pool, slipping through cool water, caressing every burnt, dried-out crack of skin. The competitive faces of my teammates shape-shifted from glaring hulks to wide-eyed clowns gearing up for a night of fun, free from the grip of competition, of wanting to be a Canadian Olympian.

I sucked the air; a fever had broken and all I could do was sweat profusely and stare at the hole in my knee, now a bloody scab. Like an automaton I followed the crowd of boisterous sweating bodies. The smell of hot food descended. Every kind of roasted meat manned by chefs ready to carve a piece, a steamy array of cooked vegetables and a salad bar the length of a football field. A series of round tables filled a far wall, each table filled with baskets of fresh fruit and manned by servers who oversaw buckets of ice cream.

Long lines formed; plates began to overflow with food. I wandered from station to station, discovering peanut butter, some fresh bread, and chicken noodle soup.

Conversations were swirling around my head—lips were moving but I could not pay attention. By now my head was vibrating with a dull pain. As I swallowed the salty soup, my right ear crackled, and then a deep ache wormed its way through my head to the other ear. It was the familiar tell-tale sign, from my grade-school days—ear infections. Allergies and ear infections went together like a hand in a glove.

I was completely undone and just needed to lie down. I left my food unfinished, somehow found my dorm room and went to bed without changing my clothes. Sleep, I just needed to sleep.

As I slept, I became vaguely aware of the pulsating cacophony of music loud and soft, fast and slow. Sometime later, the music morphed into a steady moaning, a rumble of tones that lasted for hours. The door creaked open, waking me. A disembodied head poked into the room. I thought it was a team coach; my roommate lurking behind him. He turned on the light but remained standing in the shadows and then asked where he could find some condoms.

I raised my head from the pillow and shook it side to side causing the snot to dribble from my nose. It tickled. I might have giggled; confused, snotty, and embarrassed. Had I heard what I thought I heard? I knew about condoms, a covert topic that arose during a high school biology class on reproduction, but I had never seen one, let alone known where they were kept.

Before I could say anything, the lights clicked off and the door swished closed. I fell back into bed trying to un-know what had just happened. A dark cloud had cloaked the room with cool air, raising doubts. I went back to sleep, as if what had just happened was merely a dream.

At breakfast the next morning, appetites remained large and once again plates overflowed as athletes rushed to eat as much as possible. Suitcases were piling up at the door, and the large buses that were to transport us home were arriving. Official speeches complimenting us on our hard work were muffled by the roaring buses, and the pounding of my heartbeat amplified by my snot-filled head.

"Onward to Montreal," someone shouted.

"To'76!" yelled another.

Over the next weeks and months, I wondered if that night was a fever-induced nightmare. After all, I was sick, and our team coaches were prominent men in the track and field community. Men, my father declared, who had common sense. Then the sickening memory of the sweaty face of the coach appeared.

Sport had rules, standards, and ideals that gave my life purpose; a coach having sex with his athlete was not just irresponsible, it was morally wrong. It broke every rule written or imagined.

Never in this world would I discuss this with my parents. '*I had a fever,*' was all I would say when they asked about the comfort of the dorms, and the rituals of the Olympic exhibition.

I do remember that it was around this time that my stuffed pink poodle, the one my father bought to comfort me during my bout of chickenpox, that I cuddled when the fear of losing tick-tocked its way into my dreams, was thrown out by my mother during one of her cleaning missions. She had decided that it was too old, too dirty, too stinky.

I bought a poster, 11 by 20 inches, at a library book sale and pinned it to the wall above my desk. Its background was of a gray pebbly cement section of a sidewalk with a jagged crack running diagonally across the page, an uneven path that was as black as a moonless night. A single red rose grew out of the center of the crack. Its petals perfectly folding outward with a glistening fuzzy dark green stem beneath it. The leaves on the stem held tiny raindrops the shape of tears. Gray, rose, and green—a montage of color. Effortlessly beautiful as well as a curious sight—a rose growing out of a crack in the cement, not nutritious black earth, it was a possibility.

My knee puncture healed, and the achy hamstring continued to catch fire when I ran. My allergies subsided when I got back to the hot dry air of the prairies, and I probably got antibiotics to treat my ear infections. When I added it all up, the before and the after, I knew my body had taken a beating, and my mind had gone dark.

To get to Montreal I had to deny what I had seen, and narrow my vision. Mind my own business, not get carried away, the stock phrases that I added to the book of common sense.

Every day I took stock of the beauty of the rose. It had found a way to survive.

CHAPTER EIGHTEEN

Breathlessness: The Final Race

*"I figure you're going to hurt at the end of the
race no matter what…so you might as well hurt
because you tried your hardest."*
400-meter sprinter Tim Riley

A healing muscle is at first a swampy mess. Inflammation eventually seeps away, leaving the final repair work to non-muscle cells determined to knit torn muscle with fibrous threads, layering, plastering, and gluing the ends together. If the scar forms in a willy-nilly fashion, the whole muscle will pucker and the stretching and contracting of sprinting would cause micro tears where the scar meets muscle. If, however, the athlete, meaning me, gently stretched, and received massages to the muscle, literally molding the fibrous tissue, the scar would remodel, become less thick, more pliable to sprinting. It takes time, especially when you have torn a chunk of the muscle. I had to be patient.

Mach was concerned about the persistent achiness of my hamstring muscle. Pain meant weakness. Weakness meant less power. He had massaged the torn hamstring at one of our meetings and declared that I was to spend the next season running the 400-meters, which he referred to as the longer sprint. "To run fast," he said, "but not at top speed, it will be best for the hamstring." Was he saying that my body had known gears that it could command for speed during a race? It sounded reasonable, but I had no idea how I could pace my sprinting.

The first 400 meters I ran as a sprint was probably on a Monday night in June at the Pan Am Stadium. I stood behind my blocks in an outside lane and felt weighed down by dread. Today was the day that my coach had targeted for my inaugural run. His instruction was to go out fast and then hang on. I had never done this before, and I knew it was going to hurt.

The gun sounded and my body did its thing. The first 200 meters flew by, soaring at almost top speed.

After the first 200 meters I focused on hugging the inside line of my lane, the shortest path to 400 meters. And then as I came onto the final straightaway a bluish pixelated fog started to form. My stomach contracted and vomit rose from my belly to my mouth. It burned. The muscles of my arms and then my legs hardened. My body flailing as each step became a herculean effort.

I don't remember the finish line, just the pain and the vomit and the pounding headache and everyone watching me as if this was a good thing, including my coach. He told me I ran the first 200 meters in 25.5 seconds, the last in thirty-five, a total of 60.5. 'A terrible result' is what I expected him to say. But instead, he was confident that the next time I ran 400 meters I would instinctively run a slower first 200 meters and a faster second. "Pacing," he said, "it was all about pacing."

By this time, in the fall of 1974, I had begun my second year at university studying physiotherapy in the School of Rehabilitation Science. Training and studying took up all my days. I refrained from Friday night partying to study and tried to keep up with the never-ending volume of facts that rained down with each day of classes. After my final exams of the year, I was required to work five days a week in an assigned hospital setting for the summer months. I arranged for a six-week summer internship at a hospital in Vancouver, and because I was a student athlete, the Canadian government paid for my airfare and accommodations. I had requested Vancouver so that I could also train with Gerard Mach.

The hot humid days of August compressed the air between the Rocky Mountains and the Pacific Ocean. I knew no one in Vancouver except the nurses and therapists that I saw during the day and the five other sprinters vying for a spot on the team. Mach ran the clinics and titrated my workouts to what he felt as he massaged my hamstring. He emphasized correct running habits: warm-up routines that required concentration on form, sustaining high levels of exertion with fluid movements. I enjoyed his plays on words. At times he repeated what he had always said— *'being the slowest to slow down,'*—and at other times he added a twist, *'You need*

to run good with your body,' the artifacts of my toe-walking
sensibility.

His words also resonated with what I was learning about
how the nervous system controlled movement. It gave credence
to my unconscious sense of power floating above the ground
while defying gravity. I began to feel confident that I could
run the 400 meters as a sprint. To-be-the-best-I-could-be, felt
doable. Training became a daily ritual that was a necessary
comfort, almost playful.

Before workouts, I spent the day with patients who had
severe burns, assisting my teachers and the nurses on the burn
ward with removing dressings and doing flexibility exercises
for the joints affected by the burn injuries. I was required to
wear a long cotton gowns as well as a mask and gloves, to
prevent infections that were the death knell for a burn patient.
The thick humid air smelled like pain, the hydrotherapy room
where we worked echoed with pain, and the hallways crackled
as each step hit an old, yellow, linoleum floor that refused to
lay flat.

The room where I slept was off the hallway that
connected the student dorms to the burn ward. At night, lying
in sweat, I could hear the soft groans and moans of the patients.

It was never stated in my presence but somehow, I
came to know the sadness—three patients had died from their
burns, one a four-year-old child. Pain, sleeplessness, and grief
accumulated within my body. I could not begin to find the

words to describe the suffering that swirled around my day. Going for a workout was the only time when my body could bury the miserableness that I had witnessed.

I rode a bike from my dorm to practice, a bridge between work and play that I clung onto, a spacer between suffering and soaring. I was puzzled, Mach, up until then, had seemed discouraged about the progress of my healing muscle. "Stiff," he muttered between his teeth. One day as I approached the training field, I could see him at the bike rack. And as I got closer, I could see his frowning face as his body swayed from foot to foot. I had done something wrong.

He was aghast that I would even think about riding a bike. Did I not know it would shorten my muscles, make them stiff, stop all the work of healing? And then when I mentioned it was how I could get to practice on time, that I was working in the hospital all day. He began to yell, alternating between what sounded like Polish followed by a broken English.

"Not good for your body, that to win you need to pay attention to your body, every detail of the body." He took in a breath and lowered his voice. "What you are thinking, why you would do such a thing?"

I knew the precise reasoning for riding my bike; a science argument that I thought was a good story.

"Avoid bike riding!" he said again. "Not good for muscles that then shorten and rrrripppp, when stretched by sprinting." His emphasis on the *r* of the rip felt like I was tearing the muscle all over again.

Finally, I found my words. "I go to university and I'm studying rehabilitation science to become a physiotherapist. We're learning about how to prescribe exercise to help patients recover from bad diseases like polio, arthritis, and heart attacks." I avoided telling him about the suffering I had witnessed.

"Being on your feet all day for school is not good," he said.

I wanted to add, physiotherapy was about science, not just massaging. Did he know that my ankles had the perfect distance between their center of rotation and the attachment of my Achilles tendon? Toe-walking had shaped my foot into a powerful lever of my body. Riding my bike had strengthened my quadriceps; the toe-walking had made me fast.

"Never mind this kind of university," he interrupted. "Devote yourself to running. Studying is too much for your body."

His words mocked my thinking, what I knew about the biomechanics of sprinting, about being the slowest to slow down. I felt torn—my mind had been traveling the curiosity train, but now my body was to be the only focus, to get better at sprinting, to run the 400 meters no matter what. I was to leave curiosity stalled in limbo. It was to be all about my doing.

From that day forward, I took the bus to practice and avoided bike riding. My hamstring tightened up after the forty-five-minute bus ride, and quitting university was never an option. I worked harder at everything and kept curious thinking to myself.

Over the next year I attended other training sessions whenever Mach was in Winnipeg. My mother and father were starting to talk more about my studies and often criticized my time spent training, not dressing properly in cold weather, and not eating regular meals. "Putting yourself at risk for pneumonia," was my mother's main complaint, while my father focused on my knees pounding on the cement floors. Training at the University's Gritty Grotto, which inevitably resulted in coughing fits, especially while I was sleeping, became a topic that took center stage at dinnertime conversations. "Something is not right," a constant refrain.

"It's a good thing that she's going to university, getting a good education, and preparing for a good paying job," my father said; my mother nodded.

For me, it was a constant battle between the school schedule, the demands of my professors, the physical work of training, and trying to live up to the grand vision of Gerard Mach.

I never told my parents about Mach's insistence that I quit university. And I never told them about the rumors that some of the athletes I trained with were using steroids. I recognized their oversized muscle mass, their oily skin, and their growly voices. I listened to their stories of parties, the need to blow off steam. How they were ashamed of losing all the time, and how they refused to stop smoking. I tried not to pay attention to the press as they praised these athletes—ones that were likely to be chosen to represent Canada at the 1976 Games in Montreal.

I assumed that Mach knew about the steroids and that the other national distance coaches knew about the smoking and the partying. If bike riding was forbidden to avoid injury, surely abusing a body with drugs, alcohol, and cigarettes would be too. I put my blinders on. Someone would intervene. Maybe that crisp, precise voice of June, the secretary of the Canadian Track and Field Association, would save the team from humiliation and defeat.

By now, the story of my dreams was untethered to the outside world. They were fueled by the joy and whims of toe-walking and curiosity, gut feelings that often overrode the dictums of my parents, who were fueled by fear. On some days, my dreams had begun to terrify my parents. I was nineteen years old, declared to be an Olympic hopeful by the local press, while my parents, who had never finished high school, thought I was not using my common sense.

It was after midnight when I inched my old red car into my parking spot, muting the sound of tires on gravel—a sound amplified by the stillness of the night and likely to wake my parents. I turned off the engine and blackness descended. My whole body sank into soreness from sitting and studying at the library, memorizing, and tacking up scientific facts on the invisible wall of my mind.

I looked down at my legs hidden by baggy blue polyester track pants that felt as if they had taken on a layer of fat. Two thoughts: First, was I good enough to make the Canadian Olympic team? Canadian athletes under the age of 20 were to gather in Montreal, two weeks after my final exams, to compete for spots on a team that would be chosen to compete in an international competition between Spain, Portugal, and Canada. My coach had added: making this team was important if I wanted to be considered for Montreal.

Secondly, tomorrow I would face a two-hour exam testing my knowledge of an enormous pile of facts, some of which I had not yet studied.

Failing on all fronts loomed.

I left my books on the car seat and stepped outside, carefully closing the door. Cool dampness seeped into my shoes as I chose to walk across the dewy grass and avoid the crunch of the gravel pathway. Slowly, I unlocked the door to the house. The kitchen was dark except for a cone of fluorescence from a stove light that lit up the knife, fork, and spoon marking my customary seat at the dinner table.

My stomach growled. Reaching into the fridge I found a dinner plate filled with a pile of wrinkled green peas and two slices of roast beef covered in a brown sludge that jiggled as I carried the plate to the table. I poured myself a glass of milk, making my mouth water as it slid into the glass. The first mouthfuls unleashed a variety of textures—mushy, stringy, and slimy washed down with cool sweet milk. Food sloshed around my tummy, extinguishing a dreadful hunger.

My last bites were accompanied by the whine of bedsprings and the muffled stepping of slippered feet touching down on a hallway rug. Light flooded the kitchen. My father stood at the doorway with a disapproving frown. My whole body contracted so that my words were sharp and high-pitched, "I'm not sure I can do this!"

"Do what?" he said using his why-are-you-home-so-late voice. I still could only see his face, tired but fear-filled.

"It's late, I'm tired."

Tired! He has no idea what tired feels like. For every moment of the last year, an enormous number if my mother had taken the time to multiply it out, had been scheduled, examined, timed, and mostly declared not quite good enough.

"Studying, exams, training, the Olympics!" I yelled, "It's too much!" I pounded the table with each of my words.

"You cannot do this? Now you decide you can't do this! After the money that the government invested in you! What do you mean you can't do this!"

Did he even take time to think about what my day had been? The endless pages to study, hours of sitting on hard wooden chairs, and the grinding workout. The absolute whole-body fatigue? That no-energy sense that forced me to give up on reviewing the notes, a thick mountain of pages in D-ring binders. I knew that failing the exam could derail my education.

I slammed my fork onto the table, picked up my glass of milk and gulped it back. I was failing and bone tired and now this—an angry parental face looming over me at the beloved family kitchen table because I had tried to explain how I felt like a failure.

"Use your COMMON SENSE, we've paid a lot of money for your education. Sport for Canada, taxpayers have given you money, you owe them," said my father.

He turned around and headed back to bed.

"Anyone can make your life miserable," he added with his back toward me. "You'll eventually need to get a job, don't screw your life up because your head is full of nonsense."

He walked into the dark hallway and raised his voice. "Use your GOOD SENSE."

Milky spittle leaked from my lips. Clenching my fists, now throbbing after the pounding of my words. I glared at the hallway. The familiar fear-filled stories my parents told filled the space between me and their bedroom.

My parents' *miserable memories*: not being able to take music lessons, large families all wearing each other's clothes no matter girl or boy, the mystery of how English-speaking and French-speaking and Catholic became the reason my mother sewed my school uniforms and arranged bake sales to provide money to pay for schoolbooks. Not to mention the biggies: world wars and economic depression, hunger merged with fear and worry, my mother's father dying of a heart attack when she was just a teenager. And my father's large Catholic family, a jumble of disconnected life stories that had something to do with not knowing each other because his older brothers went to war.

And then their *common sense* stories about how my mother devoted hours to cutting coupons and saving stamps from grocery shopping so that she could pick out things we needed from the catalogs. How she calculated percentages using a halting arithmetic manipulating thick numbers that she etched into paper using a pencil sharpened with a kitchen knife. She was an expert shopper.

And then there was fear, always churning and swirling around the dinner table hovering over almost every dinnertime conversation as if someone could shatter their world into a thousand useless pieces. Someone who could take IT away, because as best as I could understand, my family, including me, were not good enough—to be wary, afraid, that was their *good sense.*

The family dinner table was no longer where I belonged; I wanted to be ruled by my athleticism as if it was the only thing that made sense. My parents were afraid I would fail, no graduation, and no Olympic anything.

I wiped my face dry with the sleeve of my track jacket, gathered up my dirty dishes and threw them into the sink. I went to bed and shoehorned my thoughts into one idea. In a couple of weeks, I would compete in Montreal, make the team, travel to Portugal, and stand on the winner's podium. My mind would command my body to run fast, to be the slowest to slow down.

I would no longer entertain my parents' fears. Jobs and money were the least of my worries.

My body moving faster than anyone else was all that mattered.

I had been training for the 400-meters, learning to pace myself, which had been working. I could run twenty-seven seconds for the first 200 meters and thirty for the last. I had learned to dig deep for the last straightaway, and had continually shaved half a second off my personal best. I was at 57.3 seconds. My coach was certain I had a 56 in my body, a 26/30 split time—it would be good enough. Unbeknownst to me, my competitors had already run 55's and 54's.

I remember two things about that race. The track was perched on top of an old water reservoir that had been filled in. The St. Lawrence Seaway was nearby, and the wind howled. Chain link fences trapped old newspapers and candy wrappers. I feared that the wind would be too much for me to overcome.

I remember the end of the race, coming out of the turn onto the final straightaway—a sense of soaring as the wind now blew from behind. Sure, it hurt, but it was the hurt that I had learned to place outside of my body, to be dealt with after the finish line. I focused on being the slowest to slow down. My eyes lasering a patch of the asphalt track, ten yards past the finish line. A lonely circle of blackness that wobbled with the wind, but did not slip or slide. My body used the muscle memory of training and executed the lean, determined to erase the mistakes of the past.

My time was as predicted—56.3 seconds. I had dragged it from inside my body out into the open.

Not good enough.

Three tenths of a second too slow.

I needed to come in second.

I placed third.

After that race, at the banquet where the international team was announced, essentially future Olympians, it was clear that I had been crossed off the list. I walked around battling thoughts, seeking anything that made sense, (good or common). It started with the words on the night of the race, that I gradually put together when I eventually talked with my parents: "I did not make it." They nodded, there were no words about common sense, but I sensed their relief, and, in my mind, I assumed that they were glad that at least I had gotten a good education. They never asked whether I had passed that final exam.

And by the time I traveled back to Winnipeg, when asked what had happened by my fellow athletes, I simply said, "I did not make the team."

And then when talking with college friends as we celebrated the beginning of a school year (Indeed I had passed!), by staying up late on Friday nights, drinking wine, playing Rummoli, eating junk food, and smoking cigarillos, I might have said, if they asked, but they probably never asked, because they never exactly knew about my Olympic dreams: "I was not good enough."

Months passed. Not once did my parents mention the Olympics. All they talked about was my brother's engagement and the details of planning a wedding. I stopped training and devoted my time to schoolwork. With more time to study, and leading a normal life, I reasoned that at least as a student, it appeared that I was *'good enough.'*

And then fate intervened. I was soon to meet a man whose world view embraced curiosity, responsibility, discipline, and dedication as well as the joy found in humbleness and the chaos of single-minded pursuit. Top-down thinking fueled his curiosity, while mine grew from the ground up. In the end, we were destined to make a good team, but first, I had to shed my single-mindedness. What I had yet to learn, and what I would be forced to confront—the realities of being-the-best-that-you-can be was never about medals, podiums, and the singing of the national anthem.

CHAPTER NINETEEN

'Long Life to the Montréal Games: Longue vie aux Jeux de Montréal.'

"The Olympics do not understand Canada, and Canada does not understand the Olympics. As a result, all 22 million of us have been going around for five years with the vague feeling something is wrong with the 1976 Games."

Sportswriter Doug Gilbert

There is very little that I remember about the Montreal Games, the least of which was their motto—an ideal that would come true but in a way that mocked their efforts. The Games did indeed live a long life as they became known as the most expensive, worst fiscally-managed Games of the twentieth century. It would take thirty years before the incurred debt would be paid off, and for Canadians, the Games had failed to put a dent in the culture wars between the French and English-speaking people of Canada. A divide that had been successfully navigated between my parents given my mother's French Canadian upbringing and my father's British heritage. Curiosity, traveling, and a belief in education, embedded

in a feisty commonsensical approach to religion and day-to
-day living, was the secret to their sixty-year long marriage.
However, in my self-centered way of thinking, I thought they
could not comprehend what had been really happening around
them.

Reportedly, for the people of Quebec, it was also a time
of chaos. The budget of the Games had grown from a total of
$124 million dollars to $2.8 billion. The organizers had fallen
victim to overbidding, patronage and corruption that was then
complicated by unrest amongst construction workers. Olympic
venues were woefully behind schedule for completion in time
for the Games to begin. Securing the funds to host the Games
had become a culture war between provincial and federal
leaders. Spectators and athletes were caught in the middle.
Making the team and then winning gold medals for their side
in the war of cultural identities turned into a fierce debate
in the years prior to the Games. And security costs—no one
wanted a repeat of the Munich massacre—to fortify Montreal,
were substantial. In contrast to Munich's welcoming Olympic
village, the island city, had the trappings of an 'armed camp.'

The meaning of sport in Canada was codified, the
infrastructure to win-at-all-costs had established a foothold,
and I had turned away from athleticism, towards the science
of movement. My time to be spent on thinking about toe-
walking, the push-off, the lean, the facts of muscle injury, the
story of oxygen debt. There was to be no more living with the
joy that sprinting had brought me. I was excited to take on the

challenge of being a healthcare provider who knew a lot about movement, an expert because I had lived it from the inside out. The world of science, from what I had learned so far, seemed to resonate, make sense of what I knew, but it also felt like a playground for my curiosity.

I had gotten married in the months before the Games and moved away from home. The nightly dinnertime conversations that were once a ritual were now only held on Sundays. My mother worried that both my husband and I were starving because I had never learned to cook, so every Sunday, as we gathered with my parents, I would inevitably have some time spent by her side as she began to teach me how to cook.

But there was one Sunday when we stood at the doorway to my childhood bedroom closet.

"What do you want to do with your track suit?" my mother asked.

I remember trying to piece a thought together that made sense. It felt like I should know the answer to this question.

The track suit seemed like a long-ago story that I barely remembered. The sight of the red stripes reminded me of my colossal failure, and yet I could feel my heartbeat quicken. I remembered how it felt to be clothed in the soft cotton, as if the joy of effortlessness was a grand possibility. It must have been a long silence because she made an executive decision. She was going to pack it away in a box that would be put inside the cedar closet. It would keep it free from moths.

I sensed that my Olympic dream had not died, I agreed that the box was a good idea.

I needed time to decide on next steps. Getting back to training and competing—was it even a possibility?

CHAPTER TWENTY

Thinking About Breathlessness

"I'm learning to live; Living to learn; Starting to sing my
song; Right or wrong; Breaking away; Setting me free;
Free to be my own me…"

Singer-songwriter Beth Hart

I only discussed my plans to return to competing with my
husband and no one else. If no one knew and if I failed to
compete, I would not have to face the humiliation of failing
again. I returned to running on Churchill Drive, a memorable
location and close to the hospital where I worked. One of
my first practices with the Galaxy Track club after I had left
St. Mary's Academy was on Churchill Drive. A large grassy
boulevard that softened my footfalls accompanied by the roar
of the nearby Red River. A good place to start with general
fitness, the early dictum of my coach. Even if I never competed
again, a daily habit of running would be a win-win. I would get
fitter, and if I decided to compete, I would have a head start on
the real training. If I never competed again, I would feel *'good'*
about my body.

Churchill Drive was a mixed memory. General fitness usually started here. The practice was to involve running from pump-house to pump-house. Large red brick rectangular buildings, no windows, that had been built after the floods of 1950 to keep the river at bay. They were exactly 3.2 miles apart.

Parallel to the road, was an oversized grassy boulevard, wide enough to also serve as a make-shift football field when the need arose. The road's edge was dotted by evenly spaced streetlamps. The far edge was bounded by a stand of oak trees with mostly green leaves, some tinged yellow, all casually rustling. A bunch of swings, teeter-totters and slides were in the distance. I had always wondered about those playgrounds; the Red River was just beyond the stand of trees. From where I stood, I could hear its muffled echo—a curious lure for childhood fearlessness.

My memories went back to the first time I ran there. It was also the first meeting of my Galaxy Club teammates. They arrived dressed in short cotton running shorts, loose-fitting t-shirts, and running shoes made of leather. We eyed each other. I cringed. My thigh-length navy blue shorts, my brown-flowered cotton blouse, and my thick rubber-soled runners looked like bad choices.

"Okay, go!" The new coach yelled, and like a herd of deer, we lurched forward, a silent trampling of the spongy grass. There were some minutes where I free-floated, the grass yielding and yet lifting me forward. But then my shoulders began to heave, and my blouse tightened around my rib cage, twisting, and chafing my skin. My toes were turning numb as if I had laced my running shoes too tightly, and my legs were weighing me down. A bridge came into view. The finish line, I assumed.

"Halfway there!" someone yelled behind me as I almost came to a stop, but then quickly changed gears and started running again.

By now most of the team were in front of me. Their long strides, one after another, added distance between us. Mine were shorter, springier, spending energy bounding rather than striding. I fell further behind and soon they ran out of view. Desperation began to rise to the back of my throat along with my lunch, which I had just eaten before coming to Churchill Drive. I clenched my mouth shut and kept churning my legs. The best I could do was a jog-walk, stopping was not an option.

Finally, off in the distance, the pump-house came into view, the real finish line. It was that moment that I learned about breathlessness, a lesson that would color the trajectory of the next chapter of my running life.

I surveyed the bodies of my teammates who were now huddled in a small semi-circle: bent over at the waist, hands grasping their thighs, elbows locked so as to prop up their upper bodies. Loud gasping sounds resonated with the taut ropey strands of their neck and shoulder muscles; their whole rib cages heaving with each breath.

Numb and aching, nauseous and gasping, I jogged, stumbled, and finally halted far enough away from the team so that I could still check and recheck what their bodies were doing. I meticulously mimicked the details of their postures.

Relief descended from head to toe, a stew of achy feet, leaden muscle, noisy gasps, and the sour taste of spit-up.

It was the first time in my life when breathing hurt. I would never forget the struggle to get air, to suck it in and blow it out, a breathlessness that consumed my body, my mind cloaked in a dark fog of despair.

Miss James, a Jamaican-born physiotherapist who trained in Britain, danced her way through my professional training. She was tiny in stature with a loud whole-body laugh that accompanied her teaching about patients with severe lung disease. Her story: physiotherapists were responsible for helping patients catch their breath by using breathless positions. They are a trick of biomechanics, bending over, grasping thighs, and locking elbows so that the arms can prop up the chest cage. The muscles of the upper trunk and shoulders can then work for breathing and not for moving the arms. My anatomy professor called it the way a body could reverse the origin and insertion of muscles. Miss James called it decreasing the work of breathing. I immediately recognized it as what had become my daily training ritual for catching my breath.

Miss James was confident that we could teach patients to decrease their work of breathing. Patients who have chronic obstructive lung disease, who battled their shortness of breath after every movement, every daily activity. She also taught us to apply this strategy when the patient was short of breath even as they lay in bed, using pillows to support their upper extremities. Another recommendation that would reverse the origin and insertion of the muscles of the chest cage, decrease the work of breathing. The teaching was confident, almost joyful, a story that promised that we could magically offer relief from breathlessness.

I was skeptical. From the inside out I believed that there was something else, something heroic, that could be done. The lungs were damaged beyond the body's capability to heal. Breathless positions afforded only a brief relief, not a useful strategy to get the suffering patient moving again. I decided that I would parrot the lessons to pass the exams, but I was pretty sure that I would never use this approach with a patient.

And then I met a middle-aged man, dedicated to being outside and working the land, a lifelong smoker. He had severe lung disease and as I attended rounds with physicians, they talked about the available drugs and their side effects that they hoped would help relieve his symptoms. Over the next weeks, they tried them all. His breathlessness went on unabated. I was asked to continue to treat him, to help him cough out secretions that aggravated his breathlessness, but I felt the absolute despair of '*nothing left to offer.*' I turned to the only thing I knew to do–breathless positions. A course of action that felt like defeat, but that somehow took on a sense of urgency.

I timed my sessions with him so that he would have eaten his supper, an exhausting battle between chewing and breathlessness. His room was on the side of the hospital that overlooked the red-brown swirl of the Red River. His bed was pushed off to the side; he lived his life in a recliner. On my way to his room, I stopped at the linen closet and searched for skinny pillows for his head and thick ones that could readily form an arm-sized cradle. At the end of my night shift, forsaking the institutional assertion that I could only treat a patient once every shift, I returned to his room and rearranged his pillows.

The sour hospital smell and the yellow glow from the hallway followed me into his room but then faded, as the door closed behind me. His window came into focus. By this time of day, the Red River just outside the hospital had transformed into a shimmering mass of blackness. A backdrop for the glowing lights from office buildings as they reflected off the surface of the flowing river; stars seemingly fell to earth forming a surreal but comforting symmetry. Rows and columns of radiant bubbles of light. It felt like we were someplace magical.

"I just would like…to be able to… get some sleep," he said.

I tipped the recliner to a steeper angle, two pillows under the left arm, and three under the right, a semi-turn of his upper trunk while his legs fell on top of each other. "Feels okay," he said with a smile. My last adjustment prompted him to turn his head. He could now see the stars.

His breathing paced his words, two words, sometimes three, then a breath. Sentences accumulated like precious jewels.

"Who knew...dust from farming...could make...so much trouble?" he said.

"Everyone smokes...where I come from."

"I have lung problems...why me?"

"The smoking... affected me...different."

"I never should have...I never would have...if I knew."

"Do you smoke?"

"I tried it once," I said. "Hated it. So only once."

Then as he continued to fight for his breath, looking at the river, he said, "I'm glad...you don't...smoke."

"Others...tell others...not to smoke."

Soon after that night, someone told me before my shift was to begin that he had died in his sleep.

For many weeks I returned to Churchill Drive. I walked and jogged my way between streetlights, counting steps and taking up the breathless position. Even though I was not breathless, my body sensed relief, my mind dwelled on the magic of that night: his last precious words, the mysteriously shimmering starlight, replaying it over and over in my mind. It felt magical, not heroic, it felt like breathless positions organized and tended too, were the right thing to do.

And then one day, as I walked, I understood that the wonder of Miss James's teachings had rippled between us reaching my patient and his failing body. It was a gift, and in those moments it had allowed him to gaze outward and experience the magic of a starlit night. I imagined that he had died that way, watching the stars.

I interrogated this feeling. I sensed a surefootedness as my forefoot touched the ground, and rolled, locking my lower limb, and gently vaulting my body forward. It was the first time I put words to this feeling, not athletic toe-walking words, but hopeful, wondrous words. A steady touch, a hopeful roll, rising, and falling over the path strewn with clumps of mud, rocks of all sizes and accompanied by the whole-body joyfulness of the children as they conquered the challenges of the playground.

CHAPTER TWENTY-ONE

Aesthetic Artifacts

"The athlete enjoys his effort....He likes the constraint that
he imposes on his muscles and nerves, through which he
comes close to victory even if he manages to not achieve
it...imagine if it were to expand outward, becoming
intertwined with the joy of nature and the flights of art."
Pierre de Coubertin

For me, the decision to compete or not was not an earth-shattering moment like losing a race. I reasoned that I would know what to do when my stories aligned, and next steps became as clear as a sunlit path in a forest. But the question still remained: Should I wear my Canadian tracksuit to an upcoming indoor national competition? What would the past say about my tracksuit worn only for two weeks, that had never been to an Olympics, that had occupied space in my mind for most of my growing up years?

Coubertin developed his ideals of Olympism that had guided my own dream using symbols and rituals born of his time. He attended the many festivals of sport that were occurring throughout the UK and America, co-opting the practical details of staging his Games, but also translating what he saw into an event that symbolized his vision. He came to be known as the father of the modern Olympics, le Rénovateur, a label that inferred wisdom.

Coubertin's symbolic gestures included podiums to be constructed to acknowledge the mastery of excellence: third place would be on the lowest platform, then second, with first the highest; the Games were to be occasions for competitive artistic festivals that awarded medals similar to the ones his father entered when Coubertin was a young boy; crowning the victors with olive wreaths was a tradition that they used to remind spectators of the myths of the ancient Games, as well as the telling and retelling of the myths of the grueling marathon, first run in ancient Greece, a popular dramatic tale. He designed the Olympic flag made up of five interlocking rings to be representative of five continents (Africa, America, Asia, Europe, and Oceania). The color of the rings: red, yellow, green, blue, and black, were common to the flags of countries. With each Games, the Olympic flag, raised at the opening ceremonies and lowered at the closing ceremonies, became a symbol of brotherhood that was to rule for the duration of the Games. And then at the 1920 Games, the Olympic Oath was read, athletes pledging to uphold the ideals of sportsmanship.

The art competitions included sculpture, literature, architecture, painting, choreographed dance, and music festivals. Exhibitions and sporting events often appeared in the same stadium on the same playing fields, and like athletes, the artists received medals, honored by a grand ceremony.

At the Amsterdam Games in 1928, Bruno Balke made the demonstration team but not Germany's national team. In his autobiography, Balke proudly reveals that after the Games ended, the demonstration team toured nearby cites in Germany, Austria, Hungary, and Czechoslovakia. The two-hour program displayed individual skills for the sport of boxing, fencing, judo, and gymnastics among others. Host cities billeted and fed them. To fill the gap between seeing and doing, Coubertin promoted these displays as a unique version of storytelling that told the tale of individual skill shaped through effort—a bodily force configuring an open mind, connecting peoples across cultures.

Every four years, the host cities of the Games took up the challenge to define the meaning of Olympism as seen through their cultural lens. Artistic renderings in all its forms were the conduit to understanding and believing in Coubertin's symbolism.

My father and I loved how winning performances were celebrated with solemn rituals, and we loved the stories of how the rituals evolved during the twentieth century, vignettes often told in the broadcasts of the Games. We understood the mashup of Olympic dreams colored by curiosity and learning, travel to destination cities and foreign countries, and the tasting of nurturing foods—an example of the opportunity for athletes and spectators to join together—it was Coubertin's vision of sport and brotherhood come true.

During the twentieth century, the Games evolved into a global stage involving thousands of athletes and officials, millions of spectators and a viewing audience estimated to be in the billions. But the worlds of art and sport would eventually diverge. For Coubertin, artists derived their inspiration from the beauty of movement and the inspiration of bodily effort. For artists, who also wanted a grand stage, envisioned theirs as work not evidenced by dramatic competition but rather by a deeply contemplative lifestyle. Nothing to do with sweating or wearing loose-fitting clothing.

In 1912, the organizers of the Stockholm Games turned down Coubertin's request to hold an arts Olympiad. Swedish artists had no interest in competing over their art. The organizers focused on the spectators devising strategies to encourage attendance to the Games. They used notice boards and young buglers to announce events and keep citizens abreast of the winning athletes and countries that had amassed the most medals. They arranged for choirs and military bands to provide entertainment. Partly because of the unusual abundance of sunshine during the Games, spectators responded with rambunctious cheering as the drama of sport unfolded. The crowds spontaneously began to sing the song considered to be the true national anthem of Sweden, as well as a cheerful rendition of "For He's a Jolly Good Fellow," when the Swedish King arrived to watch the soccer match between England and Sweden. Patriotism and sportsmanship flourished.

Meanwhile, Coubertin arranged for a poetry competition in opposition to the Swedish dismissal. Prior to the Games he sent out a call for entries, presumably collecting and judging them only to declare the poem he entered, "Ode to Sport," the winner. Coubertin used a pseudonym, Hohrod and Eschbach, a fact unearthed many years later. In hindsight, one can only see this as a violation of his vision of fair play, but was also probably a clue to his blind passion. He believed in Olympism, had devoted his life to resurrecting the Games, and, by 1912, he justified doing whatever he could to achieve his ideals.

By the 1952 Games in Helsinki, the IOC had decided to allow Russia to send athletes to the Games despite the events of the cold war. The Russians negotiated their participation, demanding that their athletes—essentially paid professional soldiers re-assigned to the sport battlefield, many being coerced into taking performance enhancing drugs—be declared amateurs. Winning-at-all-costs was embedded in cold war politics, ensuring high medal counts that proved the superiority of the authoritarian lifestyle. It was only seventeen years since Coubertin had died, and the meaning of amateurism was turned inside out.

Avery Brundage, now the head of the IOC, also reasoned that the art competitions included professional artists, a violation of Coubertin's Olympic oath. He discontinued the competitions and encouraged the organization of artistic festivals that were to be divorced from the official sporting events of the Games. The art of sport, a collaboration between imagination and athleticism, which had its roots in Coubertin's dreams, now relegated to a warm-up act for the real drama of the Games.

Mascots and slogans emerged, a replacement for art competitions, which were meant to symbolize the meaning of Olympism as embraced by the host country. The Games organizers collaborated with design artists re-inventing Coubertin's desire to combine the art of athleticism and sport in modern terms. Folklore and fairytales, rooted in the culture of a host country became fertile ground where symbolic characters, usually a favored animal, would resonate with the past and ignite the imagination of spectators and athletes. Meaningful mottos became the brand of each of the Games. And once a mascot was chosen, naming competitions among the citizens of the host country were held. The hosting of the Games became a collective retelling of the past attached to the ongoing never-ending drama of sport. My father and I ate it up.

The first mascot appeared at the 1972 Munich Games—a dachshund, a popular Bavarian dog known for its endurance, tenacity, and agility. Reportedly, politicians and Olympic officials, given paper and crayons after organizational meetings, had drawn their version of the mascot. A probable source for its eventual striped pastel coloring.

Officials of the 1976 Montreal Games chose a beaver, an animal with a long story embedded in Canadian history, but also known for its patience and hard work. It was named Amik, from the Algonquin language of the Indigenous people of Canada. It was my favorite mascot.

The Moscow Games in 1980 chose Misha the Bear, which became a favorite cliché of journalists as they evoked the image of a ferocious bear as the brand of Russian athleticism. Even though Misha looked like a friendly bear, it reminded me of the pain of oxygen debt.

The LA Games of 1984 picked the obvious, Sam the Eagle, attached to the motto, *Play a Part in History*. That came to be seen as failed attempts to transcend politics that the Games had always strived to attain. Reciprocating boycotts over the war in Afghanistan, headlined by American and Russian politicians, resulted in a covert disconnect between the brand of the Games and Olympism.

Moscow had its Russian bear often placed alongside the official emblem of the Games: five Olympic rings all in red. From each ring, red parallel lines extended upward, the longest line topped by a five-pointed star evoking the image of the flag of the Kremlin. Prior to and during the Games, palatial venues entertained spectators with circus, ballet, orchestral music, and folk dance. A documentary film co-opted a stanza from Coubertin's poetry, *'O sport you are Peace.'* Ceremonies honored masters of Soviet sport, while coaches fed steroids to its current stable of soldier-athletes while altering drug testing protocols and the reporting of results or both. Spectators rumored to be prisoners bused to stadium events, booed world record performances. Officials blatantly delayed and reversed rulings and measurements so as to favor Russian athletes.

The LA Games became known for its array of new music by musicians from all over the world, most notably the birth of the "Olympic Fanfare" by John Williams. Brazilian composer Sérgio Mendes dedicated a song for the 1984 Olympic Games, called "Olympia." He assembled a one thousand voice choir of singers from regional churches schools and universities. The California Institute of Arts, a private university in Santa Barbara, organized an arts festival that ran from the beginning of June to the end of the Games in August, including dance, theater, and musical performances. A global festival of art populated the performances despite the fact that 14 Eastern Bloc countries had boycotted the LA Games. Ironically, the theme song of the Games was "Reach Out and Touch (Someone's Hand)" and its performance brought spectators of the opening ceremonies to tears. Reportedly the Soviets had refused to take the television feed of the Games, so it is not clear if Russians were watching. *'Reaching out'* foiled by authoritarian politics.

By the end of the twentieth century, not unlike the contradictions of Coubertin's legacy between art and athleticism, the branding by host cities exposed a blatant disconnect between beliefs and actions.

In the years prior to the Montreal Games, many Canadian athletes were struggling to support themselves and their training to achieve excellence. Armed with only their sense of athleticism, they were stuck in the middle.

In the days leading up to the '76 Games, Bruce Kidd, scholar and Olympian, joined anti-Games protests which met with some success in finding a foothold for the voices of athletes. However, he also was an organizer of a transnational art festival, an event that held the promise of de-escalating the culture wars between French and English Canada. At the last minute, Olympic organizers, canceled the events supposedly forced by the accumulation of a massive debt which had been the by-product of the culture wars. Later, Kidd would write about the chaos that surrounded the Montreal Games: "For Canadians, from the moment a young Quebecois ran into the stadium sharing the torch with a young Anglophone woman, the Games rekindled the spirit of a united country… for two weeks, all the contradictions seemed to stand still." Sociologist J.J. MacAloon, interviewing spectators as part of his scholarship wrote: "In the stands, about the kiosks and open spaces of Olympic Park, on the Metro, and through the night in the old city, enthusiasts shared stories, tickets, etc., with each other."

The athleticism of athletes had touched the hearts and minds of spectators.

In the year after the Montreal Games, I had forged a routine of training after work. For the most part, a relief from the stresses of a young professional in their first job, wanting to not make mistakes, but sensing that I was wiser, more capable to-be-the-best-that-I-could-be. I had planted one foot in the world of science and health care, while the other remained embedded in the world of athleticism.

Every morning, my body woke to the delicious ache of having done a hard workout. As I walked from my car to the hospital, I gulped in the fresh dewy fog formed by the roiling Red River. Entering the hospital on the way to the rehabilitation department, I was accosted by the smells of the cafeteria. Especially on the days they were making boiled stews. It never smelled like the sweetness of a bakery.

I worked on the acute side of the hospital with patients weakened from cardiorespiratory illnesses or recovering from surgeries. I began the day walking the ten flights of stairs up to the fifth floor, proud of the absence of muscular fatigue, and sensing the return of my athletic self. I grabbed a wheelchair and walked into the hospital room of my new patient.

He looked to be about my age, with red curly hair and fair skin. He was dressed in street clothes sitting in a chair beside his hospital bed as if he had been waiting for me. He carried a diagnosis that meant he would die in the near future, but he was soon to be discharged and the doctors wanted to know how far he could walk before he was overcome by breathlessness.

As soon as he saw me and the chair, he stood up and walked towards it, gripped one arm of the chair, turned, and sat down with a huff. His hands clenched around the metal armrest; knuckles turning white. Something was brewing, but I pretended not to notice. Instead, I pushed him towards the hallway and then the elevator while explaining to him that we were going to the physiotherapy gym to measure how far he could walk on the treadmill.

The skin of his neck went from pale white to red blotches that soon coalesced into an entire neck and face red with anger. When we stopped at the elevators, he turned towards me. His eyes flitted over me from head to toe, my royal blue hospital uniform decorated with colorful buttons. My mother had sewed it for me, and I had picked out those bright sunny buttons thinking they would add some measure of cheer to the smelly, gloomy hospital corridors. But on this day, I sensed them as a colossal mistake. His eyes mocked my uniform as they fixated on those tiny dots of color.

"Do you do sports?" I asked, thinking that all guys enjoyed sports.

"No!" he yelled. I decided to say nothing more.

He walked for what felt like forever on the treadmill, at least 15 minutes, and told me to stop asking him if he was out of breath, and when he pushed the off button, he let the belt come to a stop and stepped off the treadmill.

"Good to go," he said. And before I could answer, he added, "Just get me out of here."

We walked back to his room rather than use the wheelchair, which I thought he would think was a hopeful sign. I asked him about going home, betting that he would be glad to get out of the hospital. He remained wordless. Not short of breath, but I could tell he was getting tired. His pace was slowing down.

I carefully matched the pace of his walking to my own.

As we walked, I began to corral my energy, straining to be a little less athletic, not walking as though I could slip into my tippy-toed dalliance with gravity, less soaring and dashing. I instinctively willed my body to be less cheerful, bouncy, and athletic. By the time we got back to his hospital room, I was sweating. He flopped onto his bed. His body tension evaporated and only then did he appear to be short of breath. Nostrils flaring, breathing through his mouth, he waved me away. Daring me to not ask him about his breathlessness.

During that next year, I saw him in the hospital several times and then in the intensive care unit. His body was restless, and his hair remained fiery red, his eyes piercing. I met his mother who apologized for his sharp words—damn-nurses, damn-doctors, damn-medications, damn-life—a constant refrain. Some days I saw his body angled and encased in anger. And then on other days, when he looked at his mother, his body gently curved inward. His fists unfurled and their hands embraced.

By the end of that year and after deciding against wearing my tracksuit at meets, the times for my indoor races were almost a full second slower than my personal bests. Gerard Mach had attended one of the indoor meets that was a showcase for international track stars, but also one where local athletes could compete. I knew he had watched my races because he told me that I had not only put on weight, but I had lost the most important thigh lift. I could no longer float above the ground when I ran. My body told me long before I could find the words—the athletic journey had ended.

The moment came not when I was face-to face with the truth and the mischievous smile of Gerard Mach. It came when I stood on Churchill Drive and realized that my body was plagued with fatigue, refusing to muster up the energy for yet another workout. Instead, I decided to take a break, to run and jog just until I felt tired, and then stop and walk. Precisely fifty steps between streetlights, the counting a mindless mantra, running, jogging, and counting.

My mind wandered over all the good things that were happening to me, but denied to my angry patient—the tragedy of his dreams and hopes unfulfilled, the rage of being singled out by such a devastating lingering disease, the months of suffering he and his mother endured.

And as I walked and jogged, stopping, resting, and then starting, my sense of floating and soaring disappeared.

I became flat-footed. With teary eyes I breathed in the fresh air but sensed its sharp edges, I smelled the freshly cut grass and its sweet decay, I felt the sun on my face, and heard the screams of delight as a ragtag army of children attacked the playground. I swiped at my tears and wondered if they would have a chance to live their dreams.

I want to live—his body twisted with anger because he knew he would not.

I felt the rage—my body untethered from power, forever falling from its joy-filled perch, replaced by the suffering of another human being.

My mother and I stood inside her cedar closet after Sunday dinner. By now both our wedding dresses were in boxes as well as my track suit. My parents were moving out of the house, into an apartment and she wanted to know what to do with my track suit that I had worn on my trip to Europe.

We told each other stories. I had almost failed my final exam, a shocking story, but by then she knew that I had graduated, so she merely shrugged. She had packed the pearly white shawl she had crocheted for my wedding in a separate box. Not needed. I married on a warm sunny spring day. No flood waters. Grasses and trees turned my favorite shade of green. I never wore the shawl, but I told her it was beautiful.

I told her how ashamed I was at my poor performance in Europe, that I ran times that were far slower than my personal bests. How my teammates had stopped having their periods.

She nodded. Had she not always known that being an athlete was not a good thing for a young girl's body? But then again, she wistfully reminisced about watching my races, she thought it was marvelous, how I ran like a gazelle. Even when I ran that fateful race in Montreal, the wind howling, papers trapped by the chain link fence, I looked pained but had still run with grace, *'effortlessness'* that she thought was beautiful. I smiled remembering the times we spent doing laundry—she always believed that I was good enough.

And now, what to do with the tracksuit?

She wanted me to take it to my home.

It was a beautiful artifact, a word that curiously combines art with fact. A word that transcended my belief in not being good enough.

The track suit, my artifact whose softness had fueled my Olympic dream. An artifact that would have been accompanied by the national anthem. Without ever discussing it, I understood, probably had always thought, that I would stand on a podium in some foreign country and sing the Canadian anthem wearing that track suit—the thrill of victory mingling with the soft cotton as it brushed up against my sweaty body. The red maple leaf of our flag swaying in the breeze. My mother, father, and I would have probably cried. We had seen other Olympians with joyous tears as their flag rose and their anthem sung on *Wide World of Sports.*

I took the boxes back to my home. I stored the wedding dress on the top shelf of my bedroom cupboard after having joyfully stood on my tippy toes so as to tuck the box in place. I unpacked my track suit and hung it up in my closet, an artifact.

In hindsight, an artifact, its redness and whiteness, its dreams of anthems and podiums, would also become a symbol attached to a story of national shame.

CHAPTER TWENTY-TWO

Dueling Narratives Take the Global Stage: Seoul 1988

"In the name of all competitors, I promise that we shall take part in these Olympic Games, respecting and abiding by the rules that govern them, in the true spirit of sportsmanship, for the glory of sport and the honour of our teams."

The Olympic Oath, Seoul Games 1988

In 1983, Roger Jackson, the president of the Canadian Olympic Association, called upon Bruce Kidd to team up with other academics and thinkers to constitute The Olympic Academy of Canada. The team focused on addressing the challenges facing the Olympic movement: providing recommendations for opportunities for women to compete, discouraging cheating and drug doping, and one that was a high priority for Kidd, a reconciliation between the excellence in sport and best-you-can-be attitudes.

The two men had differing priorities. Jackson was an advocate for promoting excellence in sport, while Kidd believed in sport as a force for promoting sportsmanship and intercultural understanding. By now, Jackson's view had taken center stage. The Canadian federal government had already invested 3.8 million dollars in athlete assistance programs paying high-performance athletes' monthly stipends. An investment of tax dollars that attached to the idea that medalists would inspire Canadians to participate in sport and instill national pride. Government was firmly entrenched in the business of funding student athletes, including the promising sprinter, Mr. Ben Johnson.

For the next five years, the debates about the dueling narratives would take place within the sphere of the Olympic Academy. One camp questioned the high standards set by the Canadian Olympic association that athletes had to achieve to even be considered for the Olympic team. Standards that were higher than those set by the IOC and that meant many national athletes would be unable to participate in the Games. Officials were firm: the Games were not the place for losers who would inspire no one, or for those learning how to compete. Difficult-to-achieve standards would result in gold medal performances, world rankings amongst the global elite, and ultimately, a bounty of Olympic medals for Canada. Winning became the priority.

The other camp wanted to recognize the hard work of national champions. They had dedicated their lives to training and sport, that sometimes fell short of the unreasonable standards. Wasn't being the-best-that-they-could-be the priority? It was the best of Olympism that tied belief to actions and led to humanism, the root ideal of Coubertin's Olympism.

By 1988, the media became fascinated by the '*Cinderella stories of sport,*' with much of their storytelling around the

Games focused on who was likely to make a national team or to win an Olympic medal despite overwhelming odds, and the high standards of excellence. Participation in the Games for participation's sake was a secondary sound bite.

Kidd attended the 1988 Seoul Games along with a group of social scientists commissioned by the Seoul Organizing Committee to study the impact of the Olympics on culture, an idea that was framed by the motto of the Games— *'Seoul to the World, the World to Seoul.' By now,* the ideology of excellence had expanded from the no-pain-no-gain training philosophy to a competitive one that demanded that athletes isolate themselves from distractions to their winning mindset. It was customary for elite athletes to stay outside the village, living for weeks in the time zone of their competitions so that their bodies could adjust to time changes, but away from the village. It was a costly replication of routines that prepared their bodies to be in top form.

Those athletes that lived in the Olympic village reported long line-ups for cafeteria food, and a disco that played music too loud, disturbing their sleep. National teams came and went, spending time in the village around their competitions and missing either the opening or closing ceremonies, or both. The close proximity of the sport venues and the Olympic village kept the athletes cocooned in a protected area. Mass media reported on mostly world records and Olympic victories, facts that scrolled over electronic bulletin boards, a constant drum roll heralding the importance of winning.

Kidd had gone to great lengths to document the intercultural exchanges between Koreans and athletes, which were poorly attended, some canceled to avoid the distraction from winning. He also followed the story of the Youth Camp of Seoul that had given seventeen Canadian delegates an opportunity to showcase Native Canadian Culture. Youths from other countries met with the Canadians, and a familiar sense of international fellowship flowed freely, focused on creativity, art, and culture.

On the night of September 25th, during the presentation of the Youth Camps showcase, Roger Jackson and other Canadian officials were inexplicably absent. Later, Kidd would learn that they were hunkered down with IOC officials consumed by the events of that day. Canadian Ben Johnson, the gold medalist in the 100-meter sprint, had tested positive for the steroid stanozolol. Canadian officials, wakened in the early morning hours, were now called upon to manage a globalized doping scandal, an awakening that would end with the gold medal being '*stripped*' from Ben Johnson.

A remarkable factoid: If Ben Johnson had attended the opening ceremonies, he would have recited the Olympic oath pledging adherence to sportsmanship and fair play. What was going through his mind as he said those words? As the gold medal was placed around his neck, as the anthem was sung?

And then in the early morning hours, of the 27th of September, as the sun was rising, officials arrived at his dorm expecting him to give back his gold medal.

Who was face to face with Johnson in that moment when the medal went from his hands to an Olympic official? Or was it from Johnson to his coach, Charlie Francis, or to the then-president of the Canadian Olympic Committee, Roger Jackson? Or to the chef de mission, Carol Anne Letheren, the leader assigned to provide the environment that ensured excellence in competition? Or was it Gerard Mach, the head coach of the Canadian Track and Field Team? Did these leaders of Olympic sport know about Johnson's steroid use and turn their backs? Did they regret turning their backs?

Or was the medal given to a coach from Winnipeg, who was with the Seoul Olympic Team? He was a chubby, jolly guy who was involved in Winnipeg Track and Field. He was a storyteller when he was not being intense about winning.

This is how I imagine it:

The group of officials walked from a meeting room somewhere in the Olympic village to the apartment where Ben Johnson was staying. A soundless, slow, steady footfall. No words were spoken. The decision had been made; the unthinkable was going to happen.

The officials wore various modes of sports attire, probably hastily chosen. The decision had been made in the early hours of the morning—best to get it over with before the media descended. Someone fingered an Olympic pin emblematic of the Games, a popular artifact. Another official carried the box for the medal—heavy as a rock despite the absent medal. It was a hot day, so everyone was probably sweating.

As the group approached Johnson's room, they may have heard him moving around. Was he singing? He did not know what was going to happen, his mind basking in the glow of fulfilling his Olympic dream. If he was singing, they may have stood silently waiting for him to finish before they knocked. It would be the least that they could do.

Someone knocked several times.

The door opened.

Johnson stood in front of them wearing the gold medal around his neck. Other Canadian athletes stood with him, loose-bodied, everyone holding bottles of Korean beer. Their jolliness vanished with a blink of an eye, as if they had known this moment was a possibility.

"It's over," someone said.

Johnson slowly nodded.

"We have tested several samples. All positive for stanozolol. We have no choice but to take away your gold medal."

Sighs of resignation and anger would pass from the officials to the group of athletes. Some of these thoughts would become obsessed with the idea that win-at-all-costs meant not getting caught. Others fueled by humiliation—cheating violated the sacredness of the Olympic oath.

The lid to the box opened; the box extended toward Johnson.

He takes a moment to stare at his feet and then runs his fingers over the ribbon of the gold medal, and lifts it over his head for the last time. The medal slides into his hand and lays on his flattened palm, while the ribbon falls beneath his hand forming a loop that swayed for several beats.

The ending is near. Johnson slowly places the medal on top of the velvet cloth that lines the box and folds the ribbon over on itself, keeping it free from the edges of the box. The lid snaps shut. The ribbon uncrushed.

Somewhere in that room, there would have been sightings of the official track suit, its redness redder than the orangeness of mine, and the maple leaf would have been prominent. Artifacts that he would have worn on the day the gold medal had been placed around his neck. We had all watched the gold medal being placed around the neck of Ben Johnson, had heard our anthem play. We could never unhear the anthem, despite the medal now lying shuttered away in the official box of the Games.

Tears, everyone, no matter what, probably close to tears. Johnson motionless as one of his teammates reaches for the door just as the group of officials reflexively step backward. With the slowest of slow motion, the door is closed.

Ben Johnson had returned the medal without brute force, no power moves, just a slow dance into shame. It is here where my imagining hits a wall. I cannot fathom how that moment felt inside his body, power, strength, soaring, or sucking and sinking? I cannot help but wonder what he had done, what he would do with his national team tracksuit. I assume he has many. Did he ever wear it in public again? Or just in the unseeable confines of his private home?

No matter how you imagine the stripping of a gold medal, shame and chaos must have been felt, and the joyous singing of our national anthem turns into an act of non-sense.

"It was like a wake," said an IOC official who had witnessed the dance of shame.

It was a singular moment that for the world of sport was an unimaginable tragedy. Of all the times the medal has been stripped, there seems to be no record of the moment or, for that matter, the re-awarding of the medal to second place, who in this story was Carl Lewis. He too, would later admit to taking stimulants that were considered performance enhancing drugs at the US trials for Seoul. A discovery that would have disqualified him from competing in Seoul.

The 100-meter final in Seoul would become labeled by a CNN reporter: *'Ben Johnson Hero or Villain? The Dirtiest*

Race in History.' It would not only bring global humiliation and shame to Canadians, but also became the event that had exposed the dark side of win-at-all-cost attitudes, a never-ending story, told and retold, in homes, classrooms, and sports halls. A story appearing under *'This day in Sport History'* bylines. A lingering consensus—winning-at-all-costs had been defeated.

CHAPTER TWENTY-THREE

The Dubin Inquiry:
An Embodied Story About
Not Lying

"Sport plants in the body seeds of physio-psychological qualities such as coolness, confidence, decision, etc.... The educator's task is to make the seed bear fruit throughout the organism, to transpose it from a particular circumstance to a whole array of circumstances, from a special category of activities to all the individual's actions."

Pierre de Coubertin

If the Munich Games had evolved into a slow leak that let the air out of the bubble of my dreams; if the Montreal Games had extinguished my joy-filled spark of effortlessness; then surely, the scandals of the Seoul Games had successfully struck a blow to the heart of my athleticism as a worthy lifetime pursuit. Seoul, and the cheating scandal, may have been the last gasp for what I had now decided was the destructiveness of win-at-all-costs attitudes. On the horizon was the Dubin Inquiry, a year-long accumulation of stories and facts investigating what had gone wrong. Something positive loomed.

Between 1976 and 1988, ambivalence over dueling narratives allowed the culture of drug doping to quietly flourish. Athletes' dreams were squeezed by trying to achieve the very high bar set by Canadian Olympic officials and sports fans, '*more medals please*,' the clarion call. To win-at-all-costs, to access the modern training facilities and the best coaches, all required increasing amounts of money and time away from jobs and schooling. Athletes had to find innovative ways to maintain their amateur status, to support their training, and to win. Most would put their education in limbo and rely on the financial support of family and friends, or under-the-table gifts from the growing industries manufacturing sport shoes and equipment. In exchange for living expenses, clothing, and access to state-of-the-art training, the companies required the athlete deemed to have the greatest chance to win a medal, to wear their brand, and endorse their product.

The 1988 Games of Seoul left many in the world of sport with their heads spinning. The chaos started the year before when a terrorist bomb had downed a Korean aircraft killing 115 people, an act by North Korea meant to protest the IOC's decision to award Seoul the hosting of the 1988 Games.

On the one hand, the Seoul opening ceremonies highlighted the story of the torch bearer, 76-year-old Sohn Kee-Chung. He was the winner of the gold medal in the 1936 Berlin Games in the marathon, but was forced by his Japanese handlers to run under his Japanese name rather than his Korean name. As he strode into the Seoul Olympic Stadium with the relay torch his Korean name, was proudly heralded. Olympism had risen to right a wrong.

Along with Sohn Kee-Chung's appearance was the Olympic mascot, Hodori, inspired by the Korean's myths of the Amur tiger. Folktales extolled the virtues of the tiger's bravery and its noble nature, a graceful and powerful animal that protected humans against the harsh wilderness.

A large human Hodori, dressed in a full black and orange striped bodysuit, entered the stadium. As mascots are prone to do, he was a ball of gestures greeting spectators with a frantic waving of arms. Atop the head of the human tiger sat a traditional Korean hat—a Sangmo, a symbol of friendliness and hospitality. The flat hat, topped by a swiveling stick that ended in a long ribbon, was a traditional attire worn at music and dance festivals. Whenever the mascot moved his head, the ribbon of the Sangmo swirled in large circles, rippled like a huge wave, or snapped like a whip. The body language of Hodori and the rippling ribbon embodied a magical unbounded joie de vivre that was contagious.

By the end of the Games, drug doping and terrorism precipitated a global moral crisis for Olympic officials that erased the memories of all that the Seoul organizers had achieved. Canadians, who had in the moments after Ben Johnson's win joined together in a nation-wide display of pride and nationalism, fractured apart into those who supported excellence along with gold medals, and those who wanted heroic athletes who were good role models for their children. Some athletes focused on his stunning world record performance and declared that he had only dedicated himself to winning. No one could blame him for doing what he had to do to win, which was what the Canadian nation had wanted him to do.

But there were other athletes who felt vindicated by Johnson's stupendous fall from grace. They had known of Johnson's cheating and had warned Canadian Olympic officials. They had been labeled as losers because they were not good enough to make the team, or even if they did, had failed to bring home an Olympic medal. But these athletes were part of another story that history was quietly shaping, a far less dramatic story that harkened back to the core of Coubertin's Olympism. Seoul was a watershed moment when the dueling narratives took center stage, and, in the end, the defeat of winning-at-all-cost attitudes seemed to be a sure bet.

Spectators of sport struggled to comprehend what exactly had happened. National joy and jubilation had exploded in the few hours after the race. Millions had stayed up late to watch the race. I had probably slept through it. I saw it on replay. I switched channels to find more stories about the race, searching for an interview with Gerard Mach. When I heard that Johnson had won, I was happy for all that I knew about Mach. He had succeeded in giving the nation an Olympic gold medal. A Canadian proclaimed to be the fastest man on earth.

And then the media blitz became a never-ending story: Johnson, along with his coach Charlie Francis, were banned from representing Canada in international competitions; parents would report how they struggled to explain to the children that their hero was, in fact, a cheater.

Daily life screeched to a halt, but as the shock, shame, and disbelief wore off, the federal government commissioned an inquiry into the scandal. The honorable Charles Dubin, also an athlete in his youth with an Olympic dream, was to head the inquiry. The announcement came on October 5th. The hearings began on November 15th and ended eleven months later on October 3rd, 1989. It involved 119 witnesses, 295 exhibits, and 26 additional briefs, including one submitted by Bruce Kidd in collaboration with other scholars.

It took two years before the final report was released (June 26, 1990). Canadian taxpayers, including my father, watched the hearings live on TV. Everyone searching for answers, aghast that hard-earned taxpayers' money had supported a cheating athlete.

Dubin and his staff had the power to subpoena witnesses who were required to appear when called, to tell the honest truth, and to produce relevant documentation.

Witnesses were allowed to be represented by a lawyer, and they could be reimbursed for travel expenses, but failure to appear or to hand over documentation could result in a $500 fine. Under the Criminal Code of Canada, lying had consequences; perjury, a criminal offense. Dubin could also recommend criminal prosecution if he felt that the facts pointed to such a drastic action.

TV cameras and journalists from around the world recorded the events of the inquiry. Archival photos of the hearing reveal that they were held in a conference room, perhaps in a convention center, drapes hung from floor to ceiling. In the front of the room were wooden tables populated with piles of three ring binders. Lawyers, dressed unremarkably in business attire, sat beside burly looking athletes who looked uncomfortable in formal clothes, or looked as though their clothes were two sizes too small. Charles Dubin sat in a high back leather chair situated on a raised podium. A room dressed up as a courtroom, but it was never an investigation, not a place where harsh justice was to be found.

Dubin's interviews with the press were philosophical in nature, careful to not reveal what he was thinking. But pictures showed his thoughtful face as he rested his right hand on his cheek and chin. In other photos he frowned, eyebrows pinched. He looked as if he was in pain.

The athletes, coaches, and officials sat off to the left of Dubin. They faced the audience as they stood with one hand on the Bible swearing to tell the truth. And once seated, as questions were asked and answered, they neither smiled nor glared, they stared past the cameras, past the audience, boring a hole into the back wall of the room.

It was a liminal space, one foot inside the rituals of the law, the other inside the dramatic world of sport. To those testifying, it must have been a nightmare, never in their imagination had they thought they would be called to this time and place. They had dreams of being an Olympian, wearing the national uniform, hearing the national anthem sung in their honor, not a witness to shame. It was a fact; the national anthem was not sung during the investigation.

According to the lead counsel, Robert Armstrong, there was an outpouring of truth telling. One televised interview showed the passion of sprinter Angella Issajenko. She was unrepentant about her own use of steroids. She was aghast at the early stories attributed to Johnson who seemed to be blaming his coach, Charlie Francis.

Armstrong questioned the wrestlers and athletes who had competed in the throwing events. They admitted they had cheated, in gruesome detail, as they described injecting drug-free urine into their bladders so as to avoid detection. Being the first to testify, they had set a high bar for honesty for those to come. Armstrong felt that the athletes, including Ben Johnson, his coach Charlies Francis, and Issajenko, who not only told the truth but produced her personal diary, had been swayed by the brutal honesty of the wrestlers and throwers.

Charlie Francis admitted to finding a way to get steroids and have them delivered to his athletes. Athletes he had befriended as they struggled financially. He was found to be revered as a coach and mentor. He reportedly absolved Gerard Mach of knowing anything of the steroid use of the sprinters. He was clear that he never forced anyone to take the drugs, he had always given them a choice—if they wanted to compete as an elite athlete or not. He believed that in the doses that they were using, there would be no long-term ill effects. Besides, he assumed the athletes would be tested for side effects. However, athletes testified they were not.

A physician who had supplied the steroids, Dr. Jamie Astephan, testified about the ethical standards he was held to as a physician. He was clear. If he did not give the athletes the drugs, they would have gotten them some other way. He believed he was keeping athletes safe from being injured by drug pushers with no medical background. He also admitted he had no knowledge, no one did at this point in time, of the long-term side effects of steroids.

Ben Johnson's testimony was also truthful. He admitted to taking steroids, but he also claimed that he had been sabotaged by his arch enemy Carl Lewis. Over the years, this theory has emerged from time to time much like other conspiracy theories of the modern era. As each year passed, sports journalists wrote stories unearthing more evidence that pointed towards sabotage. Until finally, in 1991, Charlie Francis published *Speed Trap*, his account of the scandal. The same Charlie Francis that had been so forthcoming at the Dubin inquiry, added a curious footnote: he claimed stanozolol could not have been found in Johnson's urine that day because he had been giving Johnson a different steroid altogether. The scandal had to be a set-up.

In 2010, at the age of 62, Charlie Francis died after a five-year battle with non-Hodgkin's Lymphoma. Many of his athletes attended his funeral giving witness to their belief in his genius as a coach.

In October of 1989, a year after the race had been run, the final report was released. It was recommended that Charlie Francis be banned from receiving federal funding, a death knell to his coaching of future Olympians. But Dubin also urged that he be given the right to appeal his dismissal.

Similarly, Ben Johnson's lifetime ban that the federal government had declared, was frowned upon, hinting that such a ban could only be served by the sport governing body. Ben Johnson should also have the right of appeal.

The conduct of Dr. Astephan deserved to be investigated, and appropriate disciplinary actions taken by his professional board of ethics.

Dubin declared that there was a '*moral crisis in sport*' that even though not the purview of the inquiry, he noted that cheating had probably occurred at all levels of international sport. He criticized the Olympic movement in Canada for linking funding to medal counts. He recommended funding for sport be reformed to develop a robust system of doping control, as well as being accountable to the ideal of improving community participation in physical activity. He had a vision of sport for all, including minorities, the disabled, and disadvantaged socio-economic peoples. All of whom had probably been spectators of sport.

In his memoir, Bruce Kidd describes the double-edged sword that the Dubin inquiry faced. Kidd understood not only the emotional struggle to dream of being an Olympian, to dedicate oneself to the dictates of no-pain-no-gain, and he had seen first-hand the financial difficulties that such a dedication required. In his own career, he knew he had been lucky to have the emotional support of his family, but he also knew about the struggles of those who had to figure it out themselves.

Cheating was definitely wrong, and in his submission to the inquiry, he would not condone the use of steroids. He put the blame for the disaster that Seoul had become as part of a system that emphasized excellence over being the best-that-you-can-be. His solutions were to redirect and reprioritize the intercultural experience of the global stage as being equivalent to the excellence in sport. He grieved over the good outcomes of Seoul: the diplomatic accomplishment of full global participation, the collaboration between Paralympic and Olympic organizations, the breathtaking opening ceremonies, and, for Bruce Kidd, the meaningful performance of the Canadian Youth delegation as it presented its showcase of Native Canadian culture.

However, the Dubin inquiry has also found its legacy—those called to testify did not lie, they could have engaged in cover-up, blaming, and obfuscation. As I sifted through the words of the cheaters, the honesty of their testimonies was astonishing. Did they not lie because of their belief that their athleticism was born mostly of Francis's genius coaching? Did Dubin, an athlete in his youth, understand the roots of their competitive athleticism? His words were critical but also even handed, always prefaced by a thinly veiled empathy. Journalists who covered the public phase of the inquiry noted how Dubin went out of his way to make the athletes comfortable in their testimony.

In the end, the report was a condemnation for win-at-all-costs—it pointed toward an ideal that government funding should not be only for the elite, but should also provide taxpayer dollars directed at recreational facilities in all communities providing opportunities for all. It had been a long-forgotten premise when funding for the elite athletes was first proposed in 1969, that the Dubin inquiry now praised as a solution to this moral crisis in sport. Sport-for-all had gained a foothold.

It was a myth that everyone applauded, but the rise of the sports media complex had summited the sport edifice. It was to prove to be a formidable unrelenting force. A force that was a lifeblood for athletes but as indiscernible as the air we breathe on a peaceful moonlit night.

CHAPTER TWENTY-FOUR

'Friends for Life': Barcelona Games 1992

"In my general course of lectures on anatomy, the great authorities made no account of the knowledge derived from motions of our own frame. I called this consciousness of muscular exertion a sixth sense."

Sir Charles Bell

Barcelona hosted the 1992 Games, and as it prepared to host the global community, it transformed itself from a '*Mediterranean rustbelt into a cultural and architectural jewel.*' Post Games it became a world-leading tourist and conference destination. A record 169 countries participated, including a united Germany, and the newly independent Baltic countries that formed after the dissolution of the Soviet Union. It was a Games that lived up to its motto, '*Friends for life.*' It was a Games that seemed to signal a turning point away from win-at-all-cost attitudes towards a being-the-best-you-can-be position.

In 1992, my thirty-seventh year, I was firmly entrenched in the world of science, when I confronted the win-at-all-cost-attitude of the new community I had moved to. While watching my son's fourth grade football game, I was forced to unearth my fundamental truth, the joy of effortlessness. As I then watched my children embrace their athleticism, I would soon reason that my failure to succeed in my Olympic dream had morphed into a desire to understand the neurophysiology of sensory perception. A reasoning that resonated with the joy of effortlessness, the push-off, the art of the lean, all of it hovering over my study of sensory pathways between the spinal cord and brain. Athleticism explained by the wonder of the human body, a common sense that not only aligned my life stories but yoked them together. Top-down and bottom-up thinking resonated with all that my father had taught me about life decisions. As a child, my parents had given me the space to explore my athleticism, to feel the joy of effortlessness, and to think with common sense. Once I was out in the world, I had learned to think with the tools of science, to move with an open mind, and then to be surprised by what I had learned.

The top-down story:

Humankind has speculated for centuries about how we explain the common experience of moving about our world. Philosophers and scholars have mused about this sensibility—a common sense we are all born with that allows for the control we have over gravity.

Rene Descartes philosophized: *'I think therefore I am.'* Others of his ilk had imagined an internal soul, an effort of will, or the mind as the producer of motion ideas.

Biomechanists brought number stories to the fore, modeling the human frame, walking as an inverted pendulum that becomes a coiled spring as we break into a fast jog and then a sprint.

Sir Charles Sherrington, a twentieth century British neurophysiologist and a Nobel Prize recipient in 1932 for Physiology and Medicine, discovered that peripheral nerves had two kinds of fibers: ones that carry electrical signals from the skin and muscle to the spinal cord, as well as ones that carry signals from the spinal cord back to the muscles and skin. A coming and going that explained reflex pathways. But he also was in awe of the big picture, he was an observer-of human activity, a spectator of sport, and he had devoted his life to understanding the control of movement: "to move things is all that mankind can do, for such the sole executant is muscle, whether in whispering a syllable or in felling a forest."

The bottom-up story:

The science story crafted by Balke and others had changed the world of athletes and patients with heart disease. They had deconstructed the relationship between the heart as a pump that delivered the vital life-giving oxygen, and the skeletal muscles that sucked the molecules of oxygen transforming them into energy for muscular effort. All of it informed by their experience of extreme athletic adventures where their bodies had failed. They understood fate, but were optimistic. *'They could fix it'* was what their legacy would tell.

In 1912, James Herrick proposed victims of a heart attack be confined to bed for weeks; their EKG scrutinized for signs of impending, possibly fatal, chest pain with their every move. Bed rest became the standard of care for decades until Eisenhower, months after his heart attack, got out of bed and took on the stress of a presidential election campaign. He believed that *'when the going gets tough, the tough get going,'* relying on the wisdom of the Notre Dame football coach rather than his physicians—a well-worn cliché after the war years, which my track coach loved to announce to the world of spectators when he was the master of ceremonies at a track meet.

Paradoxically, as Balke's thinking about exercise and heart disease came online, it was the muscles of the limbs, the breathing muscles, the sensations of exertion that athletes and patients focused on. And for patients it was a big deal. A diagnosis of heart disease turned patients' lives into demanding routines that required attendance to twenty-six rehabilitation visits where their exercising was watched over like a hawk. This also included restrictions on what they could eat, the necessities of losing weight, and definitely no smoking. It was as if they had lived their whole life, accumulating the joys and pleasures of daily life, which had turned out to be the wrong kind of living.

By 1994, research was beginning to show significant benefits to modifying risk factors, including living a sedentary lifestyle. By 2009, data on over 601,099 Medicare patients arrived on the scene. Those patients, who had coronary artery disease and attended cardiac rehabilitation and secondary prevention programs, had mortality rates that were 21-34% lower when compared to patients that did not. This study among others led to the recommendation that these programs become a standard of care for patients recovering from an event caused by coronary artery disease. Medicare provided increasing reimbursement.

But then, utter astonishment. This 2009 study also revealed that the majority of patients eligible for cardiac rehabilitation did not participate. It was unconscionable; somehow a gap had formed between the hard-won successes of fixing the pump, and patients getting their life back—and it felt as big as the Grand Canyon.

One of my patients told me that he would never stop eating donuts, despite his irregular heartbeat and the likelihood of more surgery. He had tried to avoid the bakeries, driving out of his way, only to collapse on his stressful days when life's realities were bearing down, pointing him back to the emotional boost of the smell of the bakery. It was as if eating a donut, like smoking, was the only thing in his life that was good. Eating the donut was his choice as he faced more fix-it procedures, out of control blood sugars, his heart beating erratically. It was as if paying attention to the list of to-do's was worse than when the doctors and nurses and exercise physiologists took control of his body.

I collected other heart-felt, bottom-up stories. Some of my patients did not want to try. They complained they were unmotivated, plagued by memories of participating in the yearly high school track and field meet, usually on a hot sweaty day. Over life's decades they enjoyed a sedentary lifestyle, and now, after a grueling stress test, heart surgery, and more stress tests, they were expected to wear exercise clothing, a good pair of shoes, and a sweatband. Doctors and nurses telling them not to eat red meat and other high cholesterol foods like shrimp, was a tipping point into ambivalence.

Dr. Paul Dudley White, named Dr. Cardiology by *TIME* magazine in his obituary of 1973, centered his career on the story of the electrocardiogram. In his own life, he was a regular walker and bike rider, believing that this would ward off the death knell of the heart attack.

Before that, William Stokes wrote, in 1896, about a patient with chest pain who cured himself by working at his lumbering profession, every day adding more minutes of felling trees and chopping wood, an activity that we now know requires five times more oxygen than resting.

In the 1990s, the story of Sherrington and its aftermath was beginning to catch up with exercise science. The sixth sense was now known as proprioception, a sense that is grounded by an awareness of the body as it moves in space. A sense that looks inward, that explains many facets of the story of athleticism. Proprioception was now known to be a sense made up of a web of neurons that travel from muscle to brain and back again, in complicated feed-back and feed-forward loops that controlled any and all movement: toe-walking, sprinting, walking, jumping, and throwing. And when disease struck the pathways of proprioception, any and all movement vanished.

This was the story of an apprentice butcher, Ian Waterman, who in 1971, at the age of 19, came down with an infection that resulted in damage to the nerves responsible for proprioception. His muscles still worked, but he had no means of coordinating their actions. He could stand, but not walk. He would fall over if he could not literally keep an eye on the linkages of his body from head to toe. It took several years, and many stays in rehabilitation hospitals, to learn how to adapt. He replaced his proprioceptive sense with vision while taking advantage of the fact that our bones and joints, just by their precise and specific articulations, could also constrain his functional movements.

He gained his life back by watching himself move. His sixth sense never recovered. By 1991, he was gainfully employed, enjoyed a photography hobby capturing the movement of deer, one of his favorite targets, and had gotten married. His physician, Jonathon Cole, published a book detailing the science and life of Waterman, noting: "His recovery required a different embodiment, *a different body awareness*, the opposite to you and me, trusting his body became an *act of imagination* that eventually allowed him to move in space and real time."

Mr. Waterman's point of view, his journey, was "like a daily marathon, a bloody marathon." *Pride and a Daily Marathon* became the title of the book.

Thinking with the story of a marathon runner: an athlete attempting the marathon would take weeks and months to recover. Ian Waterman's journey was unfathomable; a painful one that he compared to running a *daily* marathon, no blocks of time to recover. It was the best-that-he-could-be.

Proprioception is a common sense of movement, a story with a universal theme that works on us as children as we try our hand at sport, as we fail or succeed, and as we age. It is a sense that is linked to the success of Olympians in spite of all the external scandals and tragedies that pivots around the human attraction to the drama and beauty of athleticism. It is a truth buried inside another cliché: Actions that speak louder than words…to which we could add, no matter the pain.

Coubertin surely would smile down on the legacy he has wrought—a lively wonder-filled story of athleticism, a common sense embedded in the life of humans. Many historians agree that Coubertin's story that shaped Olympism, is an ideal, which in its broadest sense, held tightly to the notion of athleticism, how a body informs a mind. Coubertin saw the Games as an event that would draw spectators and athletes together in anticipation. He had an instinct about athleticism—an embodied art that connected spectator and athlete. And, as it turns out, it is a display of our inner selves whether moving in space or watching, it reveals an expression of the inner selves that defies the forces of gravity, if only for a moment in time. Whether we are athletes that learn to harness our athleticism, patients searching to get their lives back, or spectators living within the drama of sport, it is a story that humankind is drawn to.

It is a common sense, bottom-up story told by spectators and athletes, patients, and healthcare providers—human beings thinking with stories about the joy of moving through space.

CHAPTER TWENTY-FIVE

'Share the Spirit...Dare to Dream': Sydney Games 2000

"Not everything that counts can be counted and not everything that can be counted counts."
Albert Einstein

In the years leading up to the turn of the century, the sports media complex injected millions of dollars into the staging of the Games. The 2000 Sydney Games sat on the precipice of a new century, wanting to be the host to the next grandest spectacle. It was reported that the building of a new Olympic stadium, and upgrading sports facilities as well as transportation infrastructure, came at the expense of dollars that had been earmarked for public health. Ultimately, the Games were immensely successful, an event to emulate and yet, years later, the sport structures struggled to be maintained, an outward sign of the slide of society into inactive lifestyles. A similar scenario was repeated in 2004 at the Athens Games. The spectator had been lured to the spectacle, and if anything had *not* been inspired to participate in recreational sport, a key premise of Coubertin's Olympism. And it was not only the promise of Sydney. Data was also clearly showing that the peoples of the world were living sedentary lifestyles, leading to obesity and complicating the management of chronic disease.

In the decade of the 1990s, the story of the mascots as a connection between the Games mottos and the themes emerged. In 1992, I had watched the events of Barcelona, captivated by the images of the beautiful port city that floated across TV screens. The mascot—a Cubic rendering of a Pyrenean mountain dog—added to the aesthetic ethic.

In 1996, at the Atlanta Games, I, like everyone else, puzzled over the Whatzit mascot. Shaped like a tear drop with feet and a face, Izzy, the name given to the mascot by the designers, was a mascot rooted in imagination and not folklore. It appeared to be an example of commercialism gone astray.

And then in 1998, the Festina doping scandal broke at the Tour de France, which led the way to the establishment of the World Drug Doping Agency (WADA). Its role proclaimed, "To develop, harmonize and coordinate anti-doping rules and policies across all sports and countries… key activities include scientific and social science research; education; intelligence and investigations; development of anti-doping capacity; and monitoring of compliance with the World Anti-Doping Program."

In the subsequent years, as more athletes tested positive for banned drugs, the suspensions delivered by WADA became controversial, political, and cringe worthy. In the decades leading up to the Sydney Games, the world of sport had one foot in the past, embedded in the sport of Olympism, and yet daring to dream of what the future would hold.

A country's medal count, the world records broken or just missed, the number of medals won by Olympians over many of the Games, were still counted by journalists and sports fans, and yet there was an undercurrent—the impact of the Games on the well-being of athletes was gaining a voice. The speeches of officials and athletes focused on well-being, a collective voice that implored a more humanistic rendering of Olympism. The well-being of athletes, citizens, and spectators was at stake.

As the Sydney Games approached my family was now in the grip of high school sporting events. We watched very little of the Games on TV, but there was curiosity around the three mascots: a duck-billed platypus named Syd, symbolizing water; a kookaburra named Olly, symbolizing air; and an echidna (a spiny ant-eater) named Millie symbolizing earth. This curiosity attached itself to my long-ago desire to travel, along with my Olympic dream, to Australia and New Zealand.

However, it was not only my desire to travel that linked my past to the Sydney Games. My coming-of-age as an athlete was intimately linked to dinnertime conversations, a constant drumbeat that brought together nourishing food (albeit a bit soggy), fear, and uncertainty. Would toe-walking lead to my being a cripple? Failing at school was not tolerated.

Swear words invited a shaming punishment, except for my mother, who swore in French. However, the backdrop of our conversations that occasionally came to the forefront, was a focus on my father's health.

We all knew his family history: his mother had died young, taken, he said, by a heart attack. But at first, we were afraid for his kidneys. He routinely suffered from kidney stones where he would lay in bed for days quietly moaning and groaning. "Pain! It was terrible pain," my mother would say.

One dinnertime, it was declared that his kidney problems made his blood pressure too high and that he needed to have a calm environment; no excitement, which was hard when *Wide World of Sports* was on the TV. He had to stop smoking, which he did. He had to take medicine to keep him calm—Valium, I believe—which he did until he found out that he was addicted and then disciplined himself to stop taking it and to start being a calm person.

And then he started getting chest pain.

He never had a heart attack, but the individual strands of heart muscle were getting bigger and bigger with the strain of pumping blood against his stiffening arteries. Eventually the heart muscle was too thick, making it impossible for oxygen to find its way to all the layers of muscle. Skeletal muscle hypertrophy was good for athletes who called on power and strength to do their sport, but not for cardiac muscle, whose contraction delivered oxygen to the body every second for a lifetime. Over two billion heart beats. Hypertrophy was a killer.

Some of our dinnertime conversations then began to focus on his chest pain. There was a worry that he would become a cardiac cripple. Similar to the toe-walking variety of my childhood, except not by limping, but by chest pain limiting his daily activities, going to work, playing golf, and winter vacations in California.

When I was growing up, it was a universal belief that after a coronary event, patients were put on bed rest. No exertion allowed, even going to the bathroom required assistance. After three weeks and a loss of muscle strength, patients would be allowed to gradually increase their activity. Cardiac cripples emerged, surviving the cardiac event only to be limited to household activities due to chest pain—a cruel irony of their illness.

In my early career, I had met these patients just before they were sent home from the hospital, being asked to assess just how far they could walk without chest pain. They talked to me about their pain; how and when it occurred, they wondered if this was to be the last time they would draw a breath. It was no way to live, they would tell me. Seated exercises were all that I could offer; exercises they could do and not cause THE pain. Stretching was a go-to recommendation. Their stories accompanied me as I retreated to Churchill Drive to run, jog, walk. The patient's fear of moving was the antithesis of athleticism.

But science stories were multiplying as drug companies developed new drugs, while old ones were repurposed— some to decrease the workload on the heart. It meant that the inevitability of becoming a cardiac cripple declined. With the help of these powerful drugs, patients could do more than just sit at home. My father, at one time or another, took all of these medications. Getting a life back was how my mother and father described it, a victory over the *'hardening of the arteries, and the fatal coronary.'* The headline of his story was when he had chest pain, which also continued, he believed it would never be a fatal story. He had nitroglycerin pills, and they worked every time.

Exercise scientists like Balke added to the story. He was the project director for the University of Wisconsin as part of a National Heart Disease Prevention Study funded by the federal government. For a year he exercised faculty members who were at high risk for a 'coronary,' identified by a least three risk factors such as high blood pressure, elevated serum cholesterol levels, cigarette smoking, irregular cardiac activity and being overweight. The results showed that the exercise had improved the parameters of the participants risk profile. Balke reported that the study had lasted only one year, but by its end, participants had joined together to support the program financially so that they could continue to exercise. They were motivated because, as Balke reported, they felt younger, more vigorous while having fun and socializing with their colleagues. Balke had now brought his science story to a diverse group of people: student athletes, Olympic dreamers, pilots, and astronauts, claiming victory for Olympians, safety for air travel and moon walks, and peace of mind for heart patients destined to crippledom.

In the 1950s, in Winnipeg, Dr. Morley Cohn returned from his studies at the University of Minnesota and established a cardiac surgery program at the St. Boniface General Hospital. This included providing for a stress test laboratory in the 'C' wing of St. Boniface Hospital, where monitored exercise testing was done to diagnose coronary artery disease. However, according to cardiologist Dr. Mymin, the director of the lab, patients began to regularly show up wanting to exercise while monitored. Soon the demand increased, and patients had to find another place to exercise. This was no easy task as the weather in Manitoba was below freezing for eight months of the year— an indoor facility was needed. In 1967, the Pan Am Games had left legacy facilities for athletics, one of which was in the new physical education building that was named the Gritty Grotto. It was a place not only for students, and professors, but also for patients recovering from cardiac events to walk and run. A legacy facility that became popular.

In time, the number of participants outgrew that facility. It's unhealthy air drove community leaders to begin to raise funds for a modern building, a place to exercise as part of a rehabilitation program. Completed in 1979, it was called the Rehabilitation Fitness Center, Reh-fit for short. It was here that my father began to exercise, religiously, three times a week.

The notion that exercise could prevent heart disease was growing. By now, the work of Balke had laid the foundation for the story of *'metabolic equivalents,'* (METs). I would explain this story to the cardiac patients as they healed from open-heart surgery.

"Your heart is a pump. It needs oxygen to keep on going—so when you had chest pain it was your pump saying I am running out of gas. But you can run out of gas another way. Your muscles,when they work hard, suck up oxygen like a vacuum cleaner. When they run out of gas, they can't get the oxygen fast enough,and you feel weak and tired, and everything about getting around gets harder and harder. Surgery helps fill the gas tank, so your pump works better, but exercise gets those muscles more efficient at sucking oxygen. So, METs is an oxygen number: 1 MET is how much oxygen you need at rest, 5 METs is how much you need to play a leisurely round of golf. Walking, you need 3."

For the most part, it was a story that my patients politely listened to and rejected. They preferred the story of Gunnar Borg and the rating of perceived exertion. Inevitably we set their exercise prescription according to Borg's scale, working toward a level of exertion that they called *'somewhat hard.'*

My father's cardiologist, a humble man who oversaw my father's health for 30 years, encouraged him to enroll in cardiac rehab after his bypass surgery. Three times a week. My mother thought it was a good idea; my father seemed ambivalent until he met another patient who had a stroke as a complication of her heart surgery. Over the year, he observed big changes in how far this patient could walk. At first my dad walked three to four laps for one-half a lap of the '*stroke victim.*' Then three to her one, three to her two, until they walked three together.

By the time of the Sydney Games, my father was a regular attendee to the Reh-fit center. During this time, his functional capacity, measured by his yearly stress tests, deteriorated. His distance walked was reduced to 400 meters, taking almost 45 minutes, now limited by his lower leg muscles cramping into a painful knot. Peripheral vascular disease had caught up with his coronary artery disease. The nursing staff would come onto the track to stretch and massage the sore muscles so that he could get in his 400 meters. He also had a raging rotator cuff problem that limited his sleep, but as long as he did his arm exercises at the fitness center, he could be pain free. He was proud of the fact that he did not need to take pain-pills for his shoulder and that he could still do his 400 meters.

When my parents came to Minneapolis in June of 2000 for our son's high school graduation, he was actively dying; heart disease would finally take his life. He used our main-floor bedroom to avoid stair climbing, and I had rented a four-wheeled walker for him. He didn't have joint pain and he had not fallen, but the pull-down seat on the walker allowed him to walk without worrying about having to find a place to stop and rest when his chest pain occurred, or when he had to stop to catch a breath.

The wheels of the walker rolled as he spoke, "extremely hard."

For most of the visit my father slept. But as we went from one moment to the next, I was amazed that he was still here with us. He had ridden the wave of clinical discoveries, taking advantage of the biomedical story. Certainly fearful, and yet curious, determined, and focused on taking the next step. I don't think I ever heard him complain.

As our family approached the turn of the century, dinnertime conversations evolved into connecting by phone. Our children were far away attending medical school. They remembered that their grandfather loved to drink grapefruit juice. Didn't he know that it could interfere with his statins? Statins would have been prescribed because he had high cholesterol but, ironically, he drank grapefruit juice to help him swallow his morning pills. Why had he not been told to not drink grapefruit juice? But they did tell him not to eat shrimp, a food high in cholesterol. We reminisced. When we went out for dinner he would sit staring at the menu, getting stuck on the page where shrimp was feathered in all its many forms. The time it took to order, a fingering of the page over and over, not turning it for a long time.

We also talked about how my father benefited from the evolving interventions for heart disease, and how they were also learning that drugs discovered to prevent heart muscle from thickening, arrived too late for my father to benefit.

We remembered how he had embraced rehabilitation fitness made possible by legacy facilities from the 1967 Pan Am Games. Was it possible that legacy stories will be found linked to the facilities built for the Sydney Games? Stories that could not be counted by the economic numbers that critics of the Olympics have become fond of.

But mostly we talk about his bravery coming to my son's graduation ceremonies, attending his parties, his chuckle echoing around the house, the gray ashen pallor to his face, his raspy breathlessness, and his frequent bouts of chest pain.

Technology and innovation had almost fixed it—his heart disease, the inevitability of becoming a cardiac cripple, but not quite. My mum would tell me that his heart, on the x-ray, was as big as a football. An image she had understood from the conversation with my father's cardiologist, who had come to see my father in the hospital. It was Saturday, his kidneys were shutting down, and his cardiologist had made a special trip to see my father.

As it happened, my father would die on that September night, just days before the Sydney Games were to begin. In the moments after he died, my brother and I, his wife and my husband sat with my mother in a small room on vinyl-covered hospital chairs. My gaze wandered between my mother, sitting like a statue, consumed by disbelief, and a window where I could see the shadows of the Red River, and the lights of the bridge that crossed it. The words of the cardiologist, someone said them, or maybe it was just me thinking with the story of heart disease, or maybe it was where I would start to grieve— *'his heart, as big as a football.'* Words that attached to the image of his chest X-ray, his heart enlarged, the radiologist would have written.

But I already sensed at that moment that the chest X-ray was just a part of his end-of-life story. His whole-life-story also had a big heartedness, a quality that informed his common sense and his good sense despite the miserableness of fate and the fear it caused. His whole-life-story, his legacy that we would all come to share, was about being-the-best-that-he could-be, about living with common sense.

CHAPTER TWENTY-SIX

'Inspire a Generation': London Games 2012

"Baron de Coubertin and his peculiar vision of the sporting spectacle became the global norm and a global bureaucracy, but along the way it is the story of the athletes who strove for perfect equity and who made our flesh dance, our eyes smile, and our thinking expand."

David Goldblatt

B y now, the branding of the Games had become its own ritual, an idealism that became a successful marketing tool to be exploited by rapid advances in technology. Print, radio, and television had expanded to cable TV, the internet, and social media. The size of the audience has grown exponentially from 100,000 in 1936 to an astounding 3.6 billion people as claimed by the organizers of London 2012, a number that has yet to be surpassed, although exactly how spectators are counted by officials is not clear.

The lure of the audience was especially evident by the growing aesthetic ethic to tell the story of the host nation. Possibly, the most humorous story told was at the opening ceremonies of the London Games. It recounted the beach scene, narrated by comedian Rowan Atkinson as Mr. Bean, from the Oscar winning movie *Chariots of Fire*—a movie that dramatized the story of two British sprinters and their struggle to overcome cultural norms. The musical theme also won an Oscar and was played at the medal ceremonies throughout the 2012 London Games. *'To inspire a generation,'* was the motto for the London Games that became linked to music of *Chariots of Fire*. An experience that moved its audiences: dramatic ocean scenery, the jostling crowd of runners leaving footsteps in the wet sand, and the crashing wave of orchestrated music, a perfectly aligned mash up of movement and emotion as though all dreams do come true.

However, somehow the designers of the mascot missed the mark of the London story. They developed a talisman that was more frightening than inspiring. They named it Wenlock, presumably a nod to the town of Much Wenlock in Shropshire and the story of Coubertin, who attended multi-sport games in Wenlock in his early quest to formulate the Modern Games. It was here, where Coubertin met Dr. Brooks who inspired a noble humanistic vision of sport. The London Games wanted to claim a stake hold on the origins of Coubertin's vision.

Wenlock the mascot, was an oblong shaped blob, metallic gray in color meant to symbolize the last drop of steel used to build the new Olympic stadium. A modern transportation system had also been built linking sporting venues to the financial districts of London. It was part of the London organizers' bid to renovate an industrial brownfield, fueling opportunities for a new generation—the motto of the London Games.

Wenlock's forehead was shaped like the roof of the stadium. His head held one eye which was to represent the lens of a camera, which was immediately linked, in the mind of the spectators and critical journalists, to the preponderance of CCTV cameras that now blanketed London. A one-eyed mascot symbolized the heavy security of London after the bombings of July 7, 2007, nicknamed 7/7, that killed 50 Britons. Domestic terrorists had targeted ordinary citizens in their protests over the awarding of the 2012 Games to London.

By all accounts, Wenlock reminded everyone of the terrorism that had become associated with the Games. The bombings were the second time spectators going about their day celebrating the Games had been targeted. The first was in Atlanta in 1996, when a bomber killed a mother and injured 111 spectators who were attending a music festival in Centennial Park.

Mottos, mascots, and terrorism had become a tragic trifecta for the modern Games. Symbolism, creativity, and drama had lured us all to the global stage. No one can blame Coubertin for the unrelenting suffering and grief unleashed by the terrorism that hovered over every Games since the Munich massacre. No matter how optimistic athletes and Olympic officials had been, no matter how the ideals of Olympism had been interpreted and redefined, fate had brought terrorism to their playing fields.

I remember watching *Chariots of Fire* and struggling to contain the emotions that arose within me. The controversy surrounding the remembrances of the Munich massacre, the shocking weirdness of Wenlock, and the swell of the music collided with each moment that I spent watching the Games. My father's death, a decade earlier, had led me to question my common sense and my athleticism, an inner voice that I trusted to defeat fear and uncertainty.

In 2006, my mother was diagnosed with inflammatory breast cancer. I lived in Minneapolis; she lived in Winnipeg. So, I quit my job and decided to return to school, which would give me the flexibility to travel to Winnipeg. I juggled the demands of my teenagers with school and traveling the five hundred miles to spend time with her and help with the demands of cancer care.

I enrolled in the PhD program in rehabilitation science, linking up with a scientist I had met several years before who was doing basic science research on aging muscle. She thought I was smart, but in truth, I felt like I was barely able to follow her science stories. The mountain of details I was trying to articulate as I taught physiotherapy students felt overwhelming. It was a clinical course on how to use physical agents. No one wanted to teach it because everyone hated the stories attached to physical agents, as if hot packs, short wave diathermy, and an army of electrical devices would put a dent in the story of patients getting their life back. But it was what curriculum mandates and the accreditation police expected. It was what we had to do. And it was absolutely depressing.

To get into graduate school, there was a common exam called a GRE, that a student hoping to enter the world of academia needed to excel at. It tested analytical reasoning, as well as math and verbal skills. I had disciplined myself to study, had taken a calculus course at night for a year, and re-arranged the family schedule so that one Saturday I found myself in this cold, stinky gymnasium, sitting in an uncomfortably small desk and chair answering questions about trains and boats. How long would it take for them to go from A to B if one could only travel 5 MPH, the other 20 MPH? It was a tipping point. My mind kept wading into the pool of ambivalence. I cared not about their arrival time, angry that they were now a stupid problem to be solved. I plodded my way through the test and did well enough to gain admission to graduate school.

And then one day, as I was photocopying notes for the class I was about to teach, my mentor came into the staff room and leaned against the photocopier. In her hands were the results of my GRE. I had done well enough. She read my results out loud with a commanding voice. I could tell she had changed her mind—in fact, she was probably thinking that I was not smart. And deep down, I sensed she was right. My thinking about numbers and facts and problems to solve had been uninspired. I could probably succeed, but it dawned on me with the force of a blow—I did not want to.

One good thing about my graduate program was that I had to declare a minor—I had chosen communication guided by a vague idea about writing stories that addressed the intersection between science and the daily lives of patients.

It was a winter day, probably near springtime. The streets were crusted with dried puddles of salt applied during the winter months to keep the roads free from ice.

I stood at a busy intersection waiting for the traffic lights to give me the 'go' signal. Behind me were the stoic buildings that housed the PhD program in rehabilitation science. I had just finished writing my last exam of the semester, two hours spent regurgitating the rules of logic, testing my knowledge of how to translate word problems into computer programs that would solve equations—two hours living with the story of letters and numbers, but mostly numbers, words to be erased. Whole-body fatigue, my brain shriveling, sucked dry by not moving, only thinking.

The toes inside my oversized winter boots curled over the edge of the curb.

Across the intersection, I saw the sleek look of the modern brick buildings; my literary journalism class was scheduled to begin soon. And a tickle of delight began to grow from the tip of my toes to the top of my head. I looked up and saw the red hand turn into a jaunty green walker. Time for next steps.

As if in slow motion, I stepped off the curb. By now I mostly walked flat footed, a corrected heel, toe, and push-off. But on that day, I felt the return of my familiar contact with the balls of my feet as they hit the road and rolled inward. An adult version of toe-walking. I knew its name, supinated foot falling into pronation, and then push-off. The spring in my step returning, conjuring the joy of effortlessness.

At the same time, I turned towards the stopped cars, double checking that they were not going to move. The faces of the drivers broke out into smiles and nods, they waved gloveless hands. Urging me onward. It was as if they knew what I would do next and that they agreed. It was as if they were happy for me.

I walked into the brand-new journalism school and down a flight of polished stairs. Soon I was consumed by the thrill of being surrounded by storytellers.

Somewhere during this time, I may have also entertained the echoes of *Chariots of Fire*. Within months, after many long discussions with my husband, I recognized the best-you-can-be story of that day crossing the road. My truth, it had always been about the joy of movement, curiosity, and thinking with the whole stories I encountered. I left the PhD program in rehabilitation science, enrolled in journalism school, and began to write every day, words, sentences, and paragraphs—learning from the ground up.

It had taken almost fifteen years since I had rediscovered the joy of effortlessness while listening to Joseph Campbell. By thinking of the story of the London Games, the feel of common sense and then trusting the instinct of my athletic self, I was returned to my childhood, striving to write responsible essays about sound minds and sound bodies.

CHAPTER TWENTY-SEVEN

'A New World': Rio Games 2016

"There are Olympians, and Olympic officials, but there is no Olympic public…. There are no new Olympian prophets on the horizon, nor any sign that the core of Coubertin's ideals will ever be anything but set dressing."

David Goldblatt

E ver since the first modern Games were held in 1896, a pattern to the reporting of events has been followed by journalists. At first there were unfathomable problems. It might be about the unfinished facilities, or their locations. Parts of cities leveled, houses destroyed, relocating citizens, rebuilding brownfields, or leveling ancient forests. Political and nationalistic forces became the backdrop as each Games faced down global conflicts, cold wars, terrorism, and boycotts.

Bribery, drug doping scandals, and human rights abuses have littered the playing fields of the Games,growing in number over the last decades. Stories that are no longer told behind closed doors, but stories that have found a path to center stage. The 2016 Rio Games topped the charts in displaying the dark side of win-at-all-costs, but my thinking with the story of athleticism had gained a foothold as the champion for a new world, for being the best-that-one-can-be. And I was writing what I thought.

And what I discovered as I wrote was that it seemed as if the failures of the institution and the IOC to act on its founding principles and values had only served to inspire the spirit and art of Coubertin's vision.

In 1976, two to three million people watched the Games in person. It would grow to 6 million by the end of the 20th century. In 1976 my story had been absent from the Games, but by the turn of the century, along with the billions, I would watch the Games—going from a childhood spectator, to Olympic hopeful, and back to spectator, a health-care provider and a mother infused with joy of movement.

And in that story, I had found other stories: The journalist who had witnessed the brutal repression of Mexican students, had also witnessed the feats of Bob Beamon flying through the air, of Jim Ryun's 1500-meter race. The science stories of Balke and Daniels, Sherrington and Waterman, intersected with the life of my father, my career, and my striving to live to be the best-that-one-could-be.

Harry Jerome had also been a spectator, athlete, and then spectator. He lived in St. Boniface, a suburb close to my home in Winnipeg. He had survived the devastating floods of the 1950s. I had not yet been born, but the floods were a dinnertime story my parents would tell. He moved to Vancouver where he faced racism and survived, nurtured his athleticism despite devastating injuries, and returned to competition to win gold. In 1970, he was made an Officer of the Order of Canada—an honor given by the Prime Minister to those whose actions give meaning to the Latin motto: *desiderantes meliorem patriam* (they desire a better country). Besides the statue in Stanley Park, there are buildings named after him: the Harry Jerome Community Recreation Center, The Harry Jerome Sports Center, and also an international track meet bears his name, a competition where many come to start their own athletic journey. By all accounts, these point to his belief, his desire to *'never give up'* to be the-best-that-he-could-be, reportedly a motto he adapted as a young Boy Scout— *'always do your best.'*

Most, if not all, Olympians become spectators. Taken together they also tell stories of their experience of the dueling narratives.

At the Montreal Games, 19-year-old swimmer Shirley Babashoff was thought to be headed for five gold medals for the US. Instead, she won *'only'* silver in four events beaten by East German women. She had faced their burly bodies, like I had in Germany, had swum near personal bests and still lost. She called out the drug doping ways of the East Germans, in her post competition press conferences, and was admonished for being a poor sport. By the time of her interview in 2016, the world knew that her dreams of Olympic gold had been stolen by cheaters and that the East Germans would never be stripped of their medals.

At that interview, she also told the story of the 4x100-meter freestyle relay. The team, anchored by Babashoff, swam the greatest race of their lives. They beat the East Germans for the gold medal. Somehow, they had found a way to surpass the muscle-bound East Germans whose bodies had been committed to winning at-all-costs. Babashoff's memoir tells the story of the night before that race, how the team imagined winning, over and over again. An untold story born of an Olympic dream, a power boost to their common sense. Their athleticism had elevated the best-that-one-can-be over winning-at-all-costs.

At the same 2016 interview, the story of the East German women was also told. They were now suffering the long-term side effects of steroids rooted in the inhumane treatment by coaches and politicians. Their story had gone from victory to tragedy, and the suffering was unimaginable.

By 2018, other stories similar to Babashoff's emerged. Germany's Christian Schenk revealed in his biography that he had taken steroids prior to his gold medal performance in the decathlon at the Seoul Games in 1988. Journalists interviewed David Steen who had placed third in the event and who was certain, at the time he stood on the podium, that Schenk was a drug cheater. He tells the story of the aftermath of the admission by Schenk. For Steen, he had moved on, finding solace in the fact that he had won bronze and was, '*not willing to do absolutely anything to win gold.*'

But his concern was that the IOC's response was to condemn the drug doping, but to not take away, to strip the gold medal, from Schenk. The statute of limitations had passed—a number that absolved the consequence. The IOC hoped that Schenk's subsequent depression would bolster the fight against doping. Steen wonders, *'Will there even be an asterisk?'* Would the asterisk declare—*'achieved by cheating?'*

Would it? The question hangs in the air between Steen, the journalist, and me. To watch his son, who was also a national champion, to know that doping continues to this day, that WADA seems to have lost its way in following through on cheaters, must have been a painful reminder of his own journey to-be-the-best-that-he-could-be. Steen's words take on a cutting edginess, "…that's not the lesson I want my son to learn: 'Lie like crazy, hold on as long as you can, there's a statue of limitations on cheating and lying and then you'll be OK."

When all is said and done, most athletes, some that are now parents like Steen, when asked about their careers will rely on cliché's. Sport had fueled their confidence, taught them discipline, and even in the face of devastation, it had all been worth it.

They tell stories of their lives as spectators, and when asked where they keep their medals, some due to world record performances, they'll laugh and say that the medals are hidden away, usually in kitchen drawers…the kitchen, a place where bodies are nourished, now also a place whose drawers hide Olympic medals.

I wonder about the silver medals of Shirley Babashoff. Where did she keep them? And then, where did she keep her gold medal?

I remember my track suit. It lives on the hanger in my bedroom closet. No matter where I have lived, it has been there. I have seen it almost every morning since I stood that day with my mother staring at the box tucked inside the cedar closet. Sometimes I finger its softness, and that always reminds me of the joy of soaring, defying gravity. A sense that I carried as I traveled from spectator to athlete and then back to spectator, a thread of curiosity that unraveled a lifetime of stories. Personal stories and history threaded together by common sense, or as Balke and Mach and Diem and Kidd and all the others would agree with, a sense of optimistic fatalism.

Stories told by athletes have a physicality that some mock as benign, trite, not connected to the real meaning of life, especially when Olympians-turned-spectators, almost to a person, tell the story of their hard-won medals now being hidden away in a kitchen drawer.

It seems to me that physicality becomes trite because we deny the elegance of proprioception, our sixth sense, and the power it has over our lives. We cannot move without it. It is why the hiddenness of a kitchen drawer is overshadowed by the joys and fears of Olympic dreams, of toe-walking, of watching your football-playing and gymnastics-loving children throw their whole being, body and soul, into learning to play a sport.

Sports matter, and once all is said and done, abandoning the ideals of Olympism, even though tragic, tattered, and frayed, feels wrong. We should trust our intuition and hold onto what matters; we should search for the truths no matter what we find, and then stand firm as we build a noble playing field.

Endnotes

Ode to Olympic Dreams, is a hybrid of memoir and history. A personal story that documents the collision between growing up on the Canadian prairies in a lower middle-class family, and the era when amateurism and athleticism were being reshaped by the sport-media complex and exercise science.

The choices made in writing these essays are shaped by my insights of the past *linked* to explanations of historical events by journalists, scientists, and Olympians. As you will discover, the endnotes provide the backdrop to the events I chose to honor, memorable to my coming-of age, but not a comprehensive examination of events that impacted the Olympic movement.

Historical events follow a chronological order of the Games throughout the twentieth century divided into nine epochs of time as described by sports journalist David Goldblatt (*The Games: A Global History of the Olympics*).

My personal recollections are based on memories, some that link to the aftermath of history, and others, veiled by the fog of nostalgia or that take advantage of the benefits of hindsight. These creative non-fiction essays are rooted in fact and shaped by the tenets of storytelling.

1. Discovering My Bliss

As a young girl who loves to toe-walk, I discover 'sports' despite my mother's misgivings about my toe-walking, fearing that it will make me a cripple. My father and I enjoy watching TV sports. He overrides my mother's concerns but is adamant that schoolwork comes first.

Quote: *ABC Wild World Classic "The Agony of Defeat" Vinko Bogataj interview 1974* https://www.youtube.com/watch?v=n_ZvwIFbXMM

1. Engström P, Tedroff K. The prevalence and course of idiopathic toe-walking in 5-year-old children. *Pediatrics*. Aug 2012;130(2):279-84.

2. Sobel E, Caselli MA, Velez Z. Effect of persistent toe walking on ankle equinus. Analysis of 60 idiopathic toe walkers. *J Am Podiatr Med Assoc*. Jan 1997;87(1):17-22

3. Hirsch G, Wagner B. The natural history of idiopathic toe-walking: a long-term follow-up of fourteen conservatively treated children. *Acta Paediatr*. Feb 2004;93(2):196-9.

4. Lorentzen, J., Willerslev-Olsen, M., Hüche Larsen, H., Svane, C., Forman, C., Frisk, R., Farmer, S.F., Kersting, U. and Nielsen, J.B. (2018), Feedforward neural control of toe walking in humans. J Physiol, 596: 2159-2172. https://doi.org/10.1113/JP275539

2. Olympism

The history of Coubertin's Olympism as it linked to my family's ideals of responsibility, common sense, and the desire to build a better life. The historical events revealed in this and subsequent chapters, were found in three sources authored by sociologist J.J. MacAloon, journalist D. Goldblatt, and Olympic scholar S. Loland.

Quote: from the Olympic Charter in force as from July 17 2020, p.11. Note italicized words were added by the author.

https://stillmed.olympic.org/media/Document%20 Library/OlympicOrg/General/EN-Olympic-Charter. pdf?tab=presentation

1. Balke, B. *Matters of the Heart: Adventures in Sports Medicine.* (Healthy Learning, Monterey, CA, 2007), 24-31.

2. Diem, C. https://docslib.org/doc/11221248/carl-diem-still-controversial-50-years-on

3. Goldblatt, D. *The Games: A Global History of the Olympics.* See Section One: The Grandiose and Salutary Task and Section Two: All the Fun of the Fair, (W. W. & Norton Company, New York 2016), 1-91.

4. Loland, S. https://digital.la84.org/digital/collection/ p17103coll10/id/4174/rec/33 Pierre de Coubertin's Ideology of Olympism from the Perspective of the History of Ideas. 1995.

5. MacAloon, J. J. *This Great Symbol. Pierre de Coubertin and The Origins of The Modern Games.* Chapter One. (The University of Chicago Press, Chicago 1981), 1-7.

6. MacAloon, J. J. (ed):Olympic Games and the Theory of Spectacle IN: *Rite, Drama, Festival, Spectacle.* (Institute for the Study of Human Issues, Philadelphia, 1984), 241.

7. Balke, B. In 1992, at age 85, and after struggling with his loss of athleticism including joint replacements back surgeries and the need to use crutches to manage his pain, he coined the phrase optimistic fatalism. *Matters of the Heart,* 133.

3. The Joy of Effortlessness

In my 37th year, I re-discover the joy of effortlessness associated with toe-walking, as I observe my children's early development of their athleticism.

Quote: An excerpt from Joseph Campbell: https://jcf.org/about-joseph-campbell/follow-your-bliss/

4. Holding Onto the Ideals of Olympism: Optimistic Fatalism

World Wars were a serious blow to Coubertin's vision that world peace could be fueled by the sportsmanship of Olympians. During the Cold War years, the ideals of Olympism offered survivors of the war a road to making a better life for themselves and their families. This essay introduces the untold stories of Bruno Balke and Gerard Mach as both men connected by their experiences of war and their passion for sport, took different paths, fueled by Olympism, to build a better life.

Quote: Goldblatt, D. *The Games* excerpt of Bill Collins, organizer of the Torch Relay of the London Games 1948, 210.

1. Goldblatt, D. *The Games* 35-43, 18.

2. Mach, G. https://athleticsontario.ca/gerard-mach-2/

3. Balke, B. *Heart Matters*,) 24-96.

4. Nurmi, P. https://en.wikipedia.org/wiki/Paavo_Nurmi

5. Defying Gravity: Thinking With Story

As a 15-year-old, I compete in a national track meet the same day the astronauts walked on the moon for the first time.

Globally it was a time of awe and wonder at the power of humans to defy gravity that resonates with the effortlessness of my Olympic dream. Winning seems unimportant, but soon my dreams of effortlessness are haunted by the number story of the inverse pendulum. The memory of the moonwalk morphs into a haunting nightmare about the powerlessness of the tick-tocking pendulum.

Quote: Morris, David B. *Narrative, Ethics, and Pain: Thinking with Stories* Narrative, Vol. 9, No. 1 (Jan.,2001), pp. 55-77. Published by: Ohio State University Press.

Abstract URL http://www.jstor.org/stable/20107229

1.The history of Apollo 11: https://www.nasa.gov/mission_pages/apollo/missions/apollo11.html

2. Stephen, J.T., Zeni, J.A., Winter, D. *Winter's Biomechanics and Motor Control of Human Movement. 5th edition.* See preface for discussion of first edition which was what the author was required to read as part of her university education. Wiley, Nov 2020.

3. Edwards, S. *Nightmares and the Brain*: https://hms.harvard.edu/news-events/publications-archive/brain/nightmares-brain

6. Dueling Narratives: A Matter of Priorities

This essay reveals the history of two philosophies of sport—excellence and win-at-all-costs versus the-best-you-can-be. Kidd's early life and experiences of winning and losing shape the story of his life as he works to bridge the gap between the dueling narratives.

Quote: Loland, S. *Coubertin's Ideology of Olympism,* 64.

Kidd, B. *'Critical Support' for Sport.* Routledge, London, and New York, 2014. See essay *'A New Orientation to the Olympic*

Games' Published in 1991 based on his work with the Olympic
Academy of Canada and prepared as his scholarly opinion
on how to *renovate* the Games after the drug scandal in 1988
Seoul Games. 120

1. https://www.cbc.ca/news/canada/british-columbia/
vancouver-miracle-mile-statue-runners-return-home-where-
they-first-raced-1.3146957

2. https://monumentaustralia.org.au/themes/culture/sport/
display/32505-sportsmanship/photo/8

3. Ann Francis: https://runningmagazine.ca/the-scene/bruce-
kidd-film-runner-still-cool-after-59-years/ Also, to view/
purchase the 10 min documentary see National Film Board
Web site: https://www.nfb.ca/film/runner/

4. Kidd, B. *A Runner's Journey*. See Chapter Seven: Great
Expectations. (University of Toronto Press, Toronto, Buffalo,
London 2021). 89-100.

5. Russell, F, (ed): *Playing for Change: The Continuing
Struggle for Sport and Recreation*. (University of Toronto
Press, 2015). See essays by Peter Donnelly and Michael
Atkinson, 363; & Douglas Booth 407.

7. Discovering Common Sense

The story of the nunnery, a Catholic private school that
straddled the past and the future. It is a story of how I was
influenced by Mr. Lucas, who was a competitor of Harry
Jerome, how it led to my leaving private school for public
school and joining the Galaxy track. The commonsense ethic
of my parents appears to be successful, but the chaos of the
outside world hovers.

Quote: Lowenthal, D. "History and Memory," *The Public*

Historian 19, no. 2 (1997): 30–39.
The story of Charles Tillenius: https://www.cbc.ca/news/
canada/manitoba/artist-clarence-tillenius-dies-at-98-1.1167022

8. The Art of the Lean

The story of sprinter Harry Jerome and the dedication of his statue linked to his inspiring career. The dedication was in 1988 the same year as the Seoul Games and the doping scandal of sprinter Ben Johnson. Jerome's story is one of failing to meet nationalistic expectations and then making an historic and courageous comeback.

Quote: Harry Jerome had been declared by the Canadian government to be the athlete of the century. The heading of the plaque beneath his statue was taken from the poem *The Lady of the Lake* by Sir Walter Scott.

https://www.britannica.com/topic/The-Lady-of-the-Lake. Accessed 22 April 2023.

1.The story of Harry Jerome:

Charles, N. *A Novel... Harry Jerome the World's Fastest Man*, Red Deer Press, 2017. https://www.normacharles.com/product/runner-the-life-of-harry-jerome-worlds-fastest-man/

https://www.harryjerome.com/

https://bcblackhistory.ca/harry-jerome/

https://www.cbc.ca/player/play/2331228119

2. Artistic origin of google doodle and statue: https://runningmagazine.ca/the-scene/harry-jerome-gets-a-google-doodle/

9. The Lightning Strike

The story of my connection to a severe thunderstorm while my family was on a camping trip. The memory of that storm suddenly arises and helps me to concentrate on effortlessness and not the fear of losing when I race in a national competition. I came in second because of a poor final lean, but ran a personal best, the second-best time in Canada. It is a memory, that I realized in hindsight, where I realize that I lost an important race because I failed at duplicating Jerome's artful finishing lean.

Quote: Albert Einstein. https://www.rd.com/article/albert-einstein-quotes/

https://en.wikipedia.org/wiki/Lightning

Bezodis, NE., Willwacher, S. & Salo, A.I.T. *The Biomechanics of the Track and Field Sprint Start: A Narrative Review.* Sports Medic me 49, 1345-1364 https://link.springer.com/article/10.1007/s40279-019-01138-1

10. Civil Unrest and Protests: Mexico Games 1968

The story of how I received a grant as a student athlete from the Canadian government that was beginning to become more involved in funding student athletes. The backdrop of the Mexico Games mingled with the civil rights protests that were consuming the U.S. Bob Beamon's amazing performance, and the protests by fellow black Americans Tommy Smith and John Carlos, were two events that I remembered watching on TV with my family. Stories of Harry Jerome, and Bruce Kidd are extended describing their connections to government and community. The influence of Roger Jackson, a successful Olympian who will become President of the Canadian Olympic

Association is also described. This chapter begins to explore the growing voices of athletes in the world of sport and the range of obstacles they faced.

Quote: Pierre de Coubertin, Journal of Olympic History 14 (May 2006)

1. Kidd, B. *A Runner's Journey*. See Chapter Seven: Great Expectations, 158.

2. Kidd, B. *A Runner's Journey*. See Chapter Eleven: The Olympic Project for Human Rights, 143-154.

3. How *The Guardian* Reported the Tlatelolco Massacre: https://www.theguardian.com/cities/from-the-archive-blog/2015/nov/12/guardian-mexico-tlatelolco-massacre-1968-john-rodda

4. Goldblatt, D. *The Games* See section *The Image is Still There*, 240, 262-273.

11. Win-at-All-Costs: The Science of Oxygen Delivery

This essay explores the history of the exercise science and the involvement of Bruno Balke and one of his graduate students Jack Daniels. Their research served as the backdrop to the controversies of high-altitude training and competing of the 1968 Mexico Games. Amateurism for elite athletes (Jim Ryun) was at stake. But the science story was emerging as Balke's work and his single-minded focus on the number story, in my eyes, was the basis for win-at-all-costs narrative.

Quote: Balke, B. *Heart Matters*. Testimonial by Maura Phillips Mackowski author of Testing the Limits: Aviation Medicine and the Origins of Manned Space Flight, 10.

1. Balke, B. *Heart Matters* Daughter's acknowledgement 10; Altitude training with Ryan and Roger Jackson 99-100.

2. Wrynn, AM. *A Debt was paid off in Tears Science: Science, IOC politics and the debate about high altitude in the 1968 Mexico City Olympics*, The International Journal of the History of Sport, 23:7, 1152-1172.

3. Balke, B. Nagle, FJ., Daniels, J. *Altitude and Maximum Performance in Work and Sports Activity.* JAMA 1965; 194(6):646-649. doi: 10.1001/jama.1965.03090190068016

4. Finn, A. *Mile High: How Kip Keino's 1500m gold changed running*
https://www.runnersworld.com/uk/training/motivation/a34396756/kip-keino-1968/

5. Tim Wendel 2018: https://globalsportmatters.com/1968-mexico-city-olympics/2018/10/18/despite-loss-in-1968-games-jim-ryun-set-americans-up-for-later-success/

6. Slotnik, DE. *Jim Hines, First to Sprint 100 Meters in Under 10 Seconds, dies at 76.* https://www.nytimes.com/2023/06/05/sports/olympics/jim-hines-dead.html

12. Being the-Best-You-Can-Be: The Science of Oxygen Delivery

The story of Gunnar Borg and the assessment scales he developed to measure the perception of exercise which he called the ratings of perceived exertion (RPE) The RPE scale and the story of oxygen debt would weigh on my mind as I watched the Mexico Games, adding to my fear of losing, foreshadowing my struggle to fulfill my Olympic Dream.

Quote: Borg, G. *Borg's Perceived Exertion and Pain Scales.* (Human Kinetics, Champaign, Illinois, 1998) 35.

1. Balke, B. *Matters of the Heart.* The Story of Jack Daniels'

connections to high altitude training and Jim Ryun prior to 1968 Games, 99-100

2. Beltz NM, et al: *Graded Exercise Testing Protocols for the Determination of VO$_2$max: Historical Perspectives, Progress, and Future Considerations.* Journal of Sports Medicine Volume 2016. http://dx.doi.org/10.1155/2016/3968393
3. Goldblatt, D. *The Games*, See section The Image is Still There: Spectacle versus Anti-Spectacle: Four, 262-273.
4. https://olympics.com/en/athletes/wyomia-tyus

13. Competing Against International Athletes

The meaning of toe-walking is re-visited after the shame and humiliation of my poor performances in international competition. I realized that the 'not winning' was the least of that shame. Not winning because I had failed to do my best, was worse. I doubled down on being a responsible athlete no matter the chaos of the political world and the disdain of my teammates, while recognizing that my Olympic dream was now linked to the support of my parents and community.

Quote: William Shakespeare. *The Tempest.* The line appears in Act IV, Scene 1. See analysis and summary of the play by the Shakespeare Birthplace Trust publicly funded by Arts Counsel England. https://www.shakespeare.org.uk/explore-shakespeare/shakespedia/shakespeares-plays/tempest/

14. 'Munich 1972' and Beyond (The Munich Massacre)

I retell my personal memory of following the Munich Massacre in juxtaposition to a 2016 documentary made to commemorate the untold stories of that awful day. For forty-five years the massacre has been remembered alongside the image of a masked terrorist standing on the balcony holding a rifle. The words of Andrei Spitzer and the aftermath of the massacre as told by his wife Ankie, suggest that our collective focus should be on the athletes murdered, the words of Andrei and Ankie Spitzer, rather than the politics and terrorism of a masked man.

Quote: *Munich '72 and Beyond* produced by Michael Cascio and Stephen Crisman: https://pbsinternational.org/programs/munich-72-and-beyond/

1. Paula Hancocks and Jake Kwon: https://www.cnn.com/2018/01/22/asia/north-korea-secret-agent-blew-up-plane-intl/index.html

2. Cathal Kelly, sports journalist *Toronto Star*:

https://www.thestar.com/sports/olympics/2012/04/28/kelly_munich_massacre_terrorists_helped_unwittingly_by_canadians_in_1972_olympic_atrocity.html?utm_source=share-bar&utm_medium=user&utm_campaign=user-share

3. Miller, Elhanan (July 26, 2012). PA official applauds decision to forgo 'racist' moment of silence for Munich victims. https://www.timesofisrael.com/pa-official-thanks-olympic-president-for-rejecting-moment-of-silence

4. Berger, Barbara. *Remember my Brother and the other Murdered Israeli Athletes*. August 1, 2012. https://www.haaretz.com/opinion/2012-08-01/ty-article/remember-my-olympian-brother/0000017f-f963-d318-afff-fb632ab70000

5. MacLoon, J. J. *Rite Drama,* See Olympic Games, and the Theory of Spectacle in Modern Societies 274.

6. Harriet Sherwood: https://www.theguardian.com/sport/2012/jun/26/munich-olympics-massacre-fight-for-remembrance

7. https://www.bbc.com/news/world-asia-57924111

8. Andrew Keh *In Munich, a Tribute to Israeli Athletes and Families Persistence* https://www.nytimes.com/2017/08/30/sports/olympics/munich-olympic-massacre-1972-memorial-israeli-athletes.html

9. Watch Live: Memorial for 1972 Munich Olympics Massacre Fiftieth Anniversary where German government apologizes as families of victims are awarded 28-million-dollar settlement. https://www.youtube.com/watch?v=Lj-UYcuPUXc

15. Gerard Mach: "To be the Slowest to Slow Down"

A personal story of my connection to the coaching of Gerard Mach, whose philosophy was to downplay the no-pain-no-gain philosophy of training, and to elevate power with effortlessness—a philosophy that resonated with my toe-walking sensibility, as well as my curiosity.

Quote: Albert Einstein https://www.rd.com/article/albert-einstein-quotes/

Posted by *Athletics Weekly*, June 30, 2018. Sprint Legend Irena Szewinska dies.

https://athleticsweekly.com/uncategorized/sprints-legend-irena-szewinska-dies-100302/

16. Overtraining

I double down on overtraining, (running stairways and competing in school hallways), an adoption of the no-pain-no-gain training of my coach, that linked to my desire to overcome the poor performance of Germany. The result was a severely torn hamstring. Other physical complaints emerged. My father's commonsense collides with my desire to make the national team—a growing gap between his common sense, lack of education,and my single-minded pursuit of the Olympic dream.

Quote: Albert Einstein: https://www.rd.com/article/albert-einstein-quotes/

17. The Junior Olympics: Edmonton, Alberta, August 1974

The story of a national track meet where I had to overcome external threats to doing well: allergies, accidentally pressing a spike through my knee, and a hazy memory of a coach wanting me to help him find condoms. I was shocked, but turned my focus to making the Montreal team.

Quote: MacAloon, J. J. *Rite, Drama, Festival, Spectacle*, 1.

18. Breathlessness: The Final Race

The story of the final break with my parents, and my race in Montreal where I failed to make the team to an international Junior Meet. Making that team was seen in my eyes as essential to my future of the 1976 Games. I quit training and concentrated on my studies, partying with my college friends, and meeting the man I would marry.

Quote: Sean P. Flynn https://www.washingtonpost.com/archive/local/2002/04/25/400-meter-runners-learning-to-pace-themselves/2a97fa3a-a043-4f4b-91fb-57f2b43ff7e2/

1. Jimson Lee, 2015: https://speedendurance.com/2012/11/28/hamstring-pulls-gerard-mach-revisited/

2. Chan, CW. Rudin's A. Foot Biomechanics During Walking and Running. Review article volume 69, Issue 5, P 448-461 May 1994. https://www.mayoclinicproceedings.org/article/S0025-6196(12)61642-5/fulltext

19. 'Long Life to the Montreal Games: Longue vie aux Jeux de Montréal.'

The story of the chaos of Montreal's preparations for the Games which had become a cultural war as well as an elevation of the win-at-all-costs narrative. Shortly before the Games I had gotten married, but Sunday dinner rituals were still upheld so that my mother could teach me how to cook, a skill that had been overlooked by my Olympic dream. At one of those dinners, my mother and I try to decide what to do with my track suit. An artifact of a being not good enough, and now an inkling that belonged to the-best-you-can-be-world I now enjoyed with my husband.

Quote: Kidd, B. '*Critical Support' for Sport*. (Routledge, London, and New York, 2014) excerpted quote for sportswriter Doug Gilbert. 129, 128-137.

20. Thinking about Breathlessness

The story of how the ending to my journey to re-enter competitive athletics begins deep inside the memory of breathlessness as a young athlete running 3.2 miles for the first time, and an encounter with a patient suffering severe breathlessness due to chronic obstructive lung disease. .

Quote: Beth Hart…. https://www.youtube.com/watch?v=nF2loBxux48

21. Aesthetic Artifacts

My decision to leave competitive athletics becomes embroiled with a debate about whether to wear my Canadian national track suit to an indoor meet. The tracksuit is an artifact that I link to the growth of the aesthetic ethic from Coubertin's vision to the era of brand marketing, mascots, and mottos. Combining artistry with athleticism has never, in the history of the Games, been unconditionally embraced. By the turn of the century Coubertin's symbols were co-opted by the sports media complex to attract participants to their expanding markets fueled by globalization.

Quote: Pierre de Coubertin, Olympism: Selected Writings excerpted from Chapter 4 *The Dialectic of Modern Sport,* by Bob Beamish. IN Playing for Change edited by Russell Field, (University of Toronto Press 2015) 121.

1. MacAloon, J. J. *This Great Symbol. Pierre de Coubertin and The Origins of The Modern Games.* The University of Chicago Press, Chicago 1981. xiii

2. Interview with MacAloon: https://www.npr.org/2012/07/27/157500646/sporting-art-an-olympic-event-left-by-the-wayside

3. IOC reflections on Art and Culture: https://olympics.com/ioc/the-olympic-foundation-for-culture-and-heritage/arts-and-culture

4. A brief history of Mascot design: https://www.cnn.com/style/article/olympic-games-mascot-design-history/index.html

5. Amik the beaver: https://olympics.com/en/olympic-games/montreal-1976/mascot

6. Goldblatt D. *The Games* .For the influence of the Wenlock Games on Coubertin, 33. See also 395-399 for the history of the Opening Ceremonies that describes Coubertin's aesthetic ethic.

https://olympics.com/en/news/london-2012-launches-olympic-mascot

7. Kidd, B. In *'Critical Support' for* Sport See The Culture wars of Montreal 134, which includes a reference to J. J. MacAloon.

8. Kidd, B.*A runner's Journey.* Story of the Olympic festivals associated with 1976 Games. 216-220.

22. Dueling Narratives Takes the Global Stage: Seoul 1988

An essay recounting the scandal of the Seoul Games where I imagine how the medal was stripped from Ben Johnson, an artifact of his victory taken away and put back inside the velvet boxes of the medal ceremony. The lid snapping shut. The anthem of Canada having been proudly played, never to be unheard. I wonder if he wears his tracksuit in the aftermath of the scandal.

Quote: Karl Wendl. The Olympic Oath A brief History. https://digital.la84.org/digital/collection/p17103coll10/id/3099/rec/2

1. Kidd, B. *In A Runner's Journey* . Roger Jackson and the Olympic Academy 285-290.

2. Kidd, B. *Critical Support for Sport:* Global Perspectives. See 'Seoul to the World…and the World to Seoul… Ben Johnson. Canada at the 1988 Olympics 105.

3. James Montague. *Hero or Villain: Ben Johnson and the Dirtiest race in history* https://www.cnn.com/2012/07/23/sport/olympics-2012-ben-johnson-seoul-1988-dirtiest-race/index.html

23. The Dubin Inquiry: An Emobodied Story About *Not Lying*:

The story of the Dubin inquiry. Athletes that testify at the Inquiry are seen to be extraordinarily truthful. Which begs the question why? Could it be that Olympism and athleticism are values that they hold dear after all is said and done? ? Or could it be that they want to blame the win at all costs narrative and elevate their dedication and genius of their coach Charlie Francis? I wonder if the anthem is played amongst the rituals of the investigation. Probably not .

Quote: from Loland S excerpted from The Olympic Idea. Discourses and Essays. Karl Hofman, Schorndorf 1967, 63.

1.Paula Hancocks and Jake Kwon: https://www.cnn.com/2018/01/22/asia/north-korea-secret-agent-blew-up-plane-intl/index.html

2. Information about Hodori the mascot: https://olympics.com/en/olympic-games/seoul-1988/mascot

3. Randy Harvey: https://www.latimes.com/archives/la-xpm-1989-03-01-sp-666-story.html

4. John Kryk. Robert: https://vancouversun.com/sports/hockey/dubin-inquirys-lead-counsel-calls-for-official-probe-into-junior-hockey-scandals/wcm/0bdf7ce9-7a79-4ff9-b8c9-3d10b7b47afe

5. https://publications.gc.ca/site/eng/471665/publication.html Dubin Inquiry (athlete assistance program p 33)

6. Photos of Dubin Inquiry: https://i.cbc.ca/1.4511138.1517348660!/fileImage/httpImage/image.jpg_gen/derivatives/original_780/dubin-inquiry.jpg

https://i.cbc.ca/1.4511137.1517348608!/fileImage/httpImage/image.jpg_gen/derivatives/original_780/charles-dubin.jpg

7. Obituary of Charles Dubin: https://www.cbc.ca/news/canada/toronto/charles-dubin-who-headed-inquiry-on-drugs-in-sports-dies-at-87-1.697004

https://www.cbc.ca/player/play/2411122542

8.Background information on Winnipeg coach who I imagine may have been present when Ben Johnson's medal was reclaimed by Olympic officials.

https://www.winnipegfreepress.com/breakingnews/2013/05/14/track-champion-coach-dave-lyon-dies

https://web.archive.org/web/20131206201119/http://www.halloffame.mb.ca/honoured/1991/dLyon.htm

9. Story of Issajenko's testimony, bold defense of win-at-all-costs. https://www.deseret.com/1988/10/10/18780391/runner-confesses-she-and-johnson-took-steroids

https://www.nytimes.com/1989/03/14/sports/track-star-admits-to-use-of-steroids.html

https://www.washingtonpost.com/archive/sports/1999/09/22/sprinter-issajenko-unrepentant-about-using-drugs/10d34915-e232-431f-8a2a-c715a0dcc2f6/

10. Synopsis of Charlie Francis's book *Speed Trap* https://www.amazon.com/Speed-Trap-Charlie-Francis/dp/0246137576; see also James Montague. *Hero or Villain: Ben Johnson and the dirtiest race in history* https://www.cnn.com/2012/07/23/sport/olympics-2012-ben-johnson-seoul-1988-dirtiest-race/index.html

11. Obituary of Charlie Francis: https://www.theglobeandmail.com/sports/more-sports/charlie-francis-dies-at-61/article4318832/

12. Kidd, B. *A Runner's Journey* Dubin Inquiry, 302-308. Reference to Carol Letheren 289.

13. Goldblatt, D. *The Games.* See section Things Fall Apart: Seoul Olympics.320-325.

14. Backstory on drug doping by John Weston Parry: *The Athlete's Dilemma: Sacrificing Health for Wealth and Fame.* (Roman and Littlefield, 2017).

24. 'Friends for Life': Barcelona Games 1992

An essay that describes the story of neuroscience linking participation in cardiac rehabilitation to the discovery of the sixth sense, proprioception as the common sense, common to us all. It is a turning point for the dueling narratives and my own life story of using commons sense to face life's challenges, analogous to Balke's optimistic fatalism, Mach's slowest to slow down and to the-best-you-can-be narratives.

Quote by Sir Charles Bell excerpted from Cole, J. *Pride and a Daily Marathon.*(MIT Press. 1995.) 30.

1. Goldblatt, D. *The Games.* See The Globalization of the Olympic after the Cold War. (the Barcelona Games) 343-351.

2. Yong, Ed. *An Immense World.* See Chapter 12. Every Window at Once; Uniting the Senses; Reports on the history of proprioception as a common sense. (Random House, New York 2022)

3. Suaya, JA. et al. *Use of Cardiac Rehabilitation by Medicare Beneficiaries.* https://www.ahajournals.org/doi/full/10.1161/CIRCULATIONAHA.107.701466

4. Suaya, JA. *Cardiac Rehabilitation and survival in older coronary patients.* https://www.sciencedirect.com/science/article/pii/S0735109709012224?via%3Dihub

5. White, PD. Clin. Cardiol. 14, 622-626 (1991)

6. Kavanaugh, T. *Exercise in Cardia Rehabilitation.* Br J Med 200: 34:3-6

7. Lasby, C. *Eisenhower's Heart Attack*, See chapter One (*The Nation's Number One Killer*); Chapter 4 (*Treatment and Recovery*); and Chapter Five (*When the Going gets Tough the Tough Get Going*). (University Press of Kansas, 1997.)

8. Charles Sherrington: https://www.nobelprize.org/prizes/medicine/1932/sherrington/biographical/

9. Ian Waterman story in: Cole, J. *Pride and a Daily Marathon.* See The Physiology of Cheating, 122-137. As well as The Daily Marathon 168-174.

25. 'Share the Spirit...Dare to Dream': Sydney Games 2000

An essay that describes the history of rehabilitation fitness and the end-of-life story of my father. The alignment of personal, science and best-you-can-be stories that were now shaping my life and the life of my family.

Quote: Cameron, WB. *Informed Sociology: A Causal Introduction to Sociological Thinking.* (Random House New York), 13.

1. Role of the World Doping Agency: https://www.wada-ama.org/en/who-we-are

2. Mascots of the Sydney Games: https://olympics.com/en/olympic-games/sydney-2000/mascot

3. Performance of the Happy Wanderer. https://www.youtube.com/watch?v=3Bw3L6c9KfA

4. Backstory on drug doping by John Weston Parry: *The Athlete's Dilemma: Sacrificing Health for Wealth and Fame.* Roman and Littlefield , 2017

5. Balke, B. *Matters of the Heart*. In Cardiac Rehabilitation and Prevention. p 95-96

6.Borg, G. *Perceived Exertion and Pain Scales.* 29-38.

26. 'Inspire a Generation': London Games 2012

A story of how I came to quit my PhD program in rehabilitation medicine and work towards a degree in journalism. A decision driven by my belief in the importance of telling the stories of movement, its joy, and its science, rooted in proprioception and cardiovascular physiology, as well as tied to common sense and optimistic fatalism; to Olympic dreams and to living with chronic disease.

Quote: David Goldblatt p 3.

1. Goldblatt, D. *The Games.* See The Globalization of the Olympics after the Cold War, 329-368.

2. Goldblatt, D. *The Games.* Going South: The Olympics in the New World Order, 410-429.

27. 'A New World': Rio Games 2016.

The story of athletes, who have retired from their sport, who see their Olympic journey as an exemplar of the best-that-you-can-be narrative, privileging it over win-at-all-costs., despite the impact of political boycotts and drug doping scandals.

Quote: David Goldblatt, *The Games.* p 445

1. Tom McGowan, John Sinnott, Eoghan Macguire and Shasta Darlington https://edition.cnn.com/2016/07/29/sport/olympics-2016-venues-rio-brazil-russia-ban-zika/

2. https://la84.org/shirley-babashoff-tells-story-book-signing/

3. https://www.theguardian.com/sport/2005/nov/01/athletics.gdnsport3

4. https://www.cbc.ca/sports/olympics/summer/trackandfield/steen-schenk-ioc-doping-admission-1.4818769

5. https://olympics.com/ioc/news/fundamental-changes-to-the-olympic-oath-at-tokyo-2020-opening-ceremony

In the name of the athletes.

In the name of all judges.

In the name of all the coaches and officials.

We promise to take part in these Olympic Games, respecting and abiding by the rules and in the spirit of fair play, inclusion, and equality. Together we stand in solidarity and commit ourselves to sport without doping, without cheating, without any form of discrimination. We do this for the honour of our teams, in respect for the Fundamental Principles of Olympism, and to make the world a better place.

Acknowledgments

The idea for this book began over seventeen years ago as I sat inside a modern classroom and watched as one of my journalism professors dissected my sentence. It was an example of how *not* to write. Her careful analysis took over an hour. I learned a lot that day, as it dawned on me that I was not even close to being a writer, but the idea that sport mattered had grabbed hold of my curiosity, and I was not about to let go.

I owe a heartfelt thanks to the many editors and teachers that have shared their expertise with me: Michelle Wildgen and Susanna Daniels of Madison Writers Studio; Tim Storm of Storm Writing School; Ruth Bullivant, Tamara Dean, Rebecca Jamieson, and to author Carla Albana (*Soul of a Swimmer*, the story of a young Olympian murdered in the Margaret Douglas school shooting), whose kindness and expertise was a timely inspiration. To the enthusiastic CG Sports Publishing professionals: Mike Nicloy, Taylor Brien, Nicole Wurtele, and Cejih Yung, your helpful guidance was indispensable. And finally, to my writing buddies, Erin Patrick and Sandra Rutherford, who read many versions of this story and who encouraged me to continue, when in my mind, it all seemed so impossible.

Margaret Renkl's memoir, *Late Migration,* a book I've read many times, was a revelation. She described her family as a safety net and a trampoline, which I can say was also my experience. I dedicate this book to my parents who were my safety net, and to my husband, whose gratefulness, generosity, and support rebounded alongside the many leaps my athleticism brought into our lives and the lives of our children.

About
Untold Stories
Newsletter

Storytelling has the power to connect the dots between us in ways that remind us of our human-ness. Untold stories have an added sense of mystery and surprise. These stories work on us by taking up space in our thinking, firing our imagination, and producing a meta-narrative that links the past to the present.

Everywhere I worked, as a teacher, student, leader, or follower, I found many untold stories that ripple between scientists, historians, journalists, friends and family, and present-day events.

My *Untold Stories* Newsletter will explore these and other stories—part fact, part history, part speculation—a delight in what we know, what we don't know, and what it might mean. A reflective musing focused on personal stories embodied by the events of history that have been forgotten, discarded, denied or re-written.

You can also find me on LinkedIn or my website: jpkehler.com